KT-365-664

The Return of
the *Antelope*

WILLIS HALL

Illustrated by
Rowan Barnes-Murphy

Fontana Lions

First published in Great Britain 1985
by The Bodley Head Ltd
First published in Fontana Lions 1985
8 Grafton Street, London W1X 3LA

Fontana Lions is an imprint of
Fontana Paperbacks, a division of
the Collins Publishing Group

Copyright © Willis Hall Productions Ltd 1985
Illustrations copyright © Rowan Barnes-Murphy 1985

Printed in Great Britain
by William Collins Sons & Co. Ltd, Glasgow

Conditions of Sale
This book is sold subject to the condition
that it shall not, by way of trade or otherwise,
be lent, re-sold, hired out or otherwise circulated
without the publisher's prior consent in any form of
binding or cover other than that in which it is
published and without a similar condition
including this condition being imposed
on the subsequent purchaser.

The Return of the *Antelope*

Grandfather Garstanton frowned as he stared at the image on one of the photographic plates he had just developed.

It showed two miniature people, both dressed in tattered sailors' clothing, both fully grown but neither more than fifteen centimetres tall in relation to the table-top on which they were standing.

Later, when his grandchildren had returned, he showed them the photograph. They stared at the little people in astonishment.

"Are they *real*?" asked Gerald, wide-eyed.

"They must be dolls," said Philippa, equally amazed. "But aren't they lifelike?"

"I'm blessed if I know. And I'll tell you something else that's got me up a gumtree. . ." Their grandfather paused and a knowing smile flickered across his face. "Who put you pair of imps up to it?"

I

The red and amber picnic jellies shivered slightly as a chill breeze cut suddenly across the beach, raising a tiny cloud which pitted the pink blancmange with grains of sand and whistled between the sausage-rolls.

The two children sitting on the tartan travelling-rug forced weary smiles across their faces as they stared into the lens of the cumbersome, primitive camera set on its tripod.

"Not long now, *mes amis!*" called out the bald-headed photographer with the mutton-chop whiskers, holding aloft the rubber bulb that controlled the camera's exposure shutter.

"Hurry up, Grandfather!" said the boy, the elder of the two children. "It's freezing cold."

"*And* we're famished," added the girl, enviously eyeing the sumptuous picnic spread.

"Not long now, young 'uns. Patience is a virtue. Just sit still."

"I *can't* sit still," said the girl. "I'm shivering. And my teeth are chattering."

"This is definitely the last photographic picture that we'll take today," said the old man. "No more talking now and quiet as mice." He held up a forefinger to test the breeze. "As soon as the wind drops—freeze."

"We're already frozen," said the boy.

The old man smiled. His name was Ralph Garstanton. "A nice big smile, Philippa. Chin up, Gerald. Any moment now . . ."

But just as it seemed as if the breeze was dropping, and Mr Garstanton was on the point of squeezing his exposure bulb, a shadow fell across the splendid picnic spread. The children's shoulders drooped in dismay as they glanced up at the sky and then spoke in unison.

"The sun's gone in," they said.

The Garstanton children had every reason to feel unhappy. Gerald and Philippa, aged eleven and nine respectively, had long since grown tired that day of acting as photographic models for their grandfather. They had been busily engaged in this role since early morning.

They had stood like statues on the sea-shore holding shrimping nets. They had remained still and silent on the end of the pier gazing out to sea, even though there was not a ship in sight. They had stared solemnly and without moving at a Punch-and-Judy show on the crowded sands. They had posed on the promenade beside a grizzled fisherman mending his nets.

And now, as the afternoon was slipping into evening, here they were sitting staring at a picnic tea which they were not even going to be invited to share.

The year was 1899 and camera-photography was all the thing. Ralph Garstanton, a Victorian gentleman with one eye for the up-to-date and the other for the main chance, had been one of the first of many to realize, years before, the potential in photography. He had equipped himself with a studio and masses of apparatus. This latest venture was in the up-and-coming field of postcard-photogravure. With the aid of his grandchildren he was hoping to compile an entire series of photographic seaside picture-postcards.

The children's father was a captain with Queen Victoria's gallant Fusiliers, recently posted out to India and stationed somewhere near the Khyber Pass. Their mother, as was customary, had gone with her husband. Until Captain Garstanton's tour of duty was completed, Gerald and Philippa were to live with Grandfather Garstanton. Not that the children weren't fond of their grandparent. It was just that sometimes his enthusiasm was a little too much for them.

Like now, for instance. This was supposed to be a *holiday* and, so far, they had hardly had a minute to themselves.

"Just a few seconds more, *mes braves*," pleaded Grandfather Garstanton. "It'll be sunny and bright in a couple of shakes—you'll see."

"No, it won't," argued Gerald. "It's going to pour with rain."

"Buckets and buckets," agreed Philippa. "We'll get soaked to the skin."

"Nonsense, fainthearts," said their grandfather, looking up at the sky. "That's not a *storm* cloud." But it was. And a distant rumble of thunder belied his words.

Philippa put out a hand and a large raindrop plopped into

her palm. In no time at all, more huge raindrops were pattering on to the picnic, bouncing off the jellies on to the big pork pie.

"Pack up, pack up!" cried Mr Garstanton, fearful for his camera and panicking at once. "Pack everything!"

Philippa shook her head and sighed. "We tried to tell him so," she said, exchanging a glance with Gerald.

Some minutes later, the three of them were sheltering under the friendly striped awning of a cockle-and-whelk stall on the promenade. The first few threatening drops of rain had quickly turned into a relentless downpour which was now sheeting down along the empty sea-front as far the Garstantons could see.

Grandfather Garstanton frowned as he remembered something. "Who's got the picinic hamper?" he asked.

"I thought you were carrying it?" said Gerald, turning to his sister.

Philippa shook her head. "I left it for you," she said.

"Somebody's next month's pocket-money is about to take a hefty tumble," observed Grandfather Garstanton, adding: "That picnic hamper wasn't ours to lose, y'know."

Gerald and Philippa pulled faces at each other. The picnic hamper, they both well knew, belonged to the unsmiling Miss Mincing, proprietress of 14 Khartoum Gardens, the boarding-house where they were spending this holiday.

"Come on, troops!" Grandfather Garstanton called out suddenly. "The rain's easing off. Let's run for it!" And, clutching his clumsy camera and tripod in both hands, he set off along the promenade at a respectable trot.

Sarah Mincing peered out through the net curtains at her parlour window, sucked in her cheeks, drew her dark eyebrows close together and made disapproving clicking noises with her tongue. "They're coming back at last," she said to her housemaid, Millie, who was hovering close at hand. Then, after consulting the cameo watch on her crisp black dress, she continued with a frown: "Three minutes late and soaking wet. No consideration whatsoever for other people's household time-tables—*or* for dripping rain-water all over their freshly scrubbed hallway tiles, I'll be bound! Well, don't just stand there with your mouth open, girl! Fetch cloths!"

"Yes, 'm," said the housemaid, bobbing her mistress a hurried curtsy before scuttling out of the parlour.

Mr Garstanton and his two grandchildren came in through the stained-glass panelled front door to find themselves confronted by Miss Mincing, tight-lipped as always and energetically thumping a small brass dinner-gong.

"Your evening meal will be served on your usual table, Mr Garstanton," said Miss Mincing icily, stepping to one side to dodge Millie who had just reappeared from the kitchen with several mopping-up cloths and a bucket.

"Apologies for our unpunctuality, Miss Mincing," said Mr Garstanton. "We'll be down as soon as we've changed into dry clothes."

"As you please—it'll be *your* broth going cold. I don't have to remind you, Mr Garstanton, do I, that we do insist on having the dining-room cleared by half past six o'clock *every* evening?" Sarah Mincing paused and frowned as Mr Gar-

9

stanton bundled his tripod (though not his precious camera) into the elephant's-foot umbrella stand. "I sincerely hope it isn't your intention to leave your apparatus in my hall *all* night? This is a holiday establishment, Mr Garstanton—not a commercial business-house."

"I am most dreadfully sorry," mumbled the old photographer, lifting the camera-tripod out of the elephant's-foot umbrella stand and contriving, as he did so, almost to fall over his own feet. "I did wonder, Miss Mincing, whether I might impose upon your generosity further?"

"You and your grandchildren are my *guests*, Mr Garstanton," said Miss Mincing, as if she were the kindest, warmest, most wonderful boarding-house keeper in the world. "What can I do for you?"

"I'd like to avail myself of the dark of your cellar again after dinner," said Grandfather Garstanton. "I've several photographic plates that I'd like to develop and—"

"If you must, Mr Garstanton," said Miss Mincing, brusquely cutting him short in her usual sharp tones. "If you must. But you will see to it, I hope, that all doors and windows are kept firmly shut throughout this time?"

"I will indeed, ma'am," said the photographer, backing towards the stairs.

But Sarah Mincing was not going to allow her guest to get away with past misdemeanours quite that easily. "The odour of chemicals still pervades the parlour from your past experiments—and there was a distinct taste of something odd in the cabinet pudding at luncheon," she said, and added: "We must consider the other guests."

Philippa, standing with her brother halfway up the flight of stairs, turned to him and spoke in a fierce whisper. "What other guests? There *aren't* any other guests."

"I know," replied Gerald, dolefully. "Who'd be stupid enough to stay in this place—at this time of year—except us?"

As Mr Garstanton ushered the children up to the bedrooms to change for dinner, Gerald's spirits rose slightly as he realized that Miss Mincing hadn't noticed that the picnic hamper hadn't been returned. Perhaps Philippa and himself might have an opportunity of recovering the hamper from the sea-shore after they had finished their evening meal?

The dining-room at 14 Khartoum Gardens, like every other room in the boarding-house, was over-furnished, heavily curtained and dark and gloomy. A huge potted aspidistra stood on a whatnot in front of the window, shutting out most of the light. Two shabby stuffed owls gazed solemnly down from under glass domes on the plush-fringed mantelpiece.

The Garstantons, the only occupants of the room, were seated around their corner table. Grandfather Garstanton was still toying manfully with his bowl of thin soup which had bits of cabbage swimming in it, but the children had already pushed their plates aside untouched.

"It's not *too* bad, y'know," said their grandfather, unconvincingly. "A trifle on the tepid side, perhaps—but otherwise quite palatable . . ."

Gerald and Philippa raised their eyebrows at each other but said nothing. A moment later, Grandfather Garstanton sighed, admitting defeat, and put down his soup spoon.

Millie, who had been peering at them from around the half-open kitchen door, sprinted into the room to collect their soup plates. It occurred to Gerald that Millie did everything on the run.

"If you ask me," observed the housemaid to no one in particular, "I don't think we've seen the back of the bad weather yet. Not by a long chalk." Then, without waiting for a reply, she scuttled back into the kitchen scattering drops of soup.

Gerald and Philippa considered the significance of Millie's remark and stared at each other, glumly, across the table.

"Do we *have* to stay all week, Grandfather?" asked Gerald.

"Can't we go home tomorrow?" added Philippa.

"Go *home*?" exclaimed their grandfather, as if they had asked to be transported to the moon. "Go home *tomorrow*? I say! Steady the Buffs! Why do you want to go home? You're on your holidays!"

"Some hols," muttered Gerald under his breath.

Grandfather Garstanton took in their sorrowful expressions and fiddled with his fork. It had not been, he was forced to admit to himself, the best of holidays for the two children. "I'll tell you what, troops," he announced. "If I manage to sell the picture-postcard publishers my *At the Seaside* photogravure set, there'll be enough cash in the kitty for us all to spend next Easter at the Grand Hotel. Cheer up!"

The children managed wan smiles.

It was at this point that Millie sped back into the dining-room carrying a tray on which was balanced their main course. She put a plate in front of each of them.

"It's cold mutton," the housemaid told them. "Miss Mincing says it wants eating up. The thunder sends it off." Millie paused to glance past the luxuriant aspidistra out of the window and then added, ominously: "If you want my opinion, for what it's worth, I think we've got more bad weather still to come."

Millie was right.

Within the hour, driving rain was lashing the window-panes. The darkening evening sky was split with lightning and the heavy rumble of thunder seemed to shake the very foundations of the boarding-house. One thing was certain: there was no possibility of the children returning to the beach that evening to look for the missing picnic hamper.

Mr Garstanton had taken himself off to the cellar in order to develop his photographic plates while Gerald and Philippa were left to amuse themselves in the parlour of the boarding-house.

But the parlour was every bit as uninviting and as gloomy as the dining-room—gloomier, perhaps, at that hour of the evening when lit only by the glow of a single oil-lamp which stood on a lace tablecloth in the centre of a polished dark-wood table. There were flickering shadows everywhere. A stuffed red fox peered out from a glass-fronted case on the sideboard while an equally lifeless stoat stood with arched back in a smaller case on a pedestal by the empty fireplace.

Another bolt of lightning, nearer this time, crackled outside the window and Philippa, huddled on a horsehair sofa, jumped with fright.

"Would you like me to find something I can read to you?" asked Gerald, solicitously, standing by a bookcase he had discovered in a corner of the room.

Philippa nodded and her brother ran a forefinger along the spines of the volumes on the bookshelves.

"*Great Expectations?*"

Philippa shook her head.

"*Uncle Tom's Cabin?*"

"No, thank you."

"*The Tempest?*"

"Very funny."

"Here's one—*Under The Greenwood Tree.*"

"Has it got Maid Marion in it?" asked Philippa.

Gerald took the book down, scanned several pages and then looked doubtful. "I don't think that it's even got Robin Hood in it," he said. He put it back on the shelf and then reeled off a number of titles: "*The Heart of Midlothian? Pilgrim's Progress? The History of Henry Esmond, Esquire? Hereward the Wake? The Canterbury Tales? The Heir of Redclyffe?*"

But to each one in turn, Philippa only shook her head.

"You're just saying 'no' to everything," said Gerald.

"Only because you're not suggesting anything that sounds interesting."

"We're not looking for something interesting, Phil. We're trying to find something that will take your mind off the thunder and lightning. How about *Barchester Towers?*"

"No, thanks."

Gerald sighed. "If you don't say 'yes' to something soon, I'll just choose something *I* want to read and I'll read it to myself."

"What else is there?"

"*Gulliver's Travels?*"

As Gerald read out the title there was an enormous flash of lightning right outside the window accompanied simultaneously by a crash of thunder louder than any that had gone before.

"Yes, please!" said Philippa, almost jumping out of her skin.

Some distance away, all along the sea-front, the howling wind lashed the sea into a green-black frenzy, causing high spume-filled waves to smash down along the empty rain-swept promenade and beat hard against the iron stanchions under the pier.

"*It would not be proper to trouble the reader with the particulars of our adventures in those seas,*" Gerald read aloud to his sister in the circle of light from the oil-lamp, "*let it suffice to inform him that, in our passage from thence to the East Indies, the good ship 'Antelope' was driven by a violent storm to the north-west of Van Diemen's Land—*" He broke off as Philippa jumped nervously again at another flash of lightning followed by the crash of thunder. "I'm sure that wasn't as close as the last one, Phil," he said.

Philippa nodded her head, firmly. "It *was!*" she said. "I'm sure it was!"

"I'll prove to you that the storm is moving away from here."

"How?"

"By counting the seconds between the lightning and thunder. Next time there's a lightning-flash we'll count together." Gerald's eyes went back to the open copy of *Gulliver's Travels* and, again, he began to read aloud. "*The seamen spied a rock, within half a cable's length of the ship—but the wind was so strong that we were driven directly upon it, and our vessel immediately split. Six of the crew, of whom I was one, let down the boat into the sea. We therefore entrusted ourselves to the mercy of the waves—*"

Once again the parlour was lit from outside by a shaft of lightning. But Gerald had been right. The storm *was* moving away. This time the lightning-flash was not immediately accompanied by thunder.

The children began to count off seconds together: "One— two—three—four . . ."

2

On the morning after the storm, Gerald and Philippa went down to the cove before breakfast, while the beach was still deserted, to look for the lost picnic hamper. Not that they had much hope of finding it.

"It's probably miles and miles away by now," said Gerald, kicking at the sand disconsolately. "It'll have been swept out to sea in last night's storm."

"Shows how much you know, Mr Know-It-All," cried Philippa, giving a little jump of joy. "*Look!*"

Gerald's eyes followed Philippa's pointing finger and he was surprised to see the picnic hamper, some fifty or sixty metres away, safe on the shore and wedged between two rocks. The wickerwork hamper was resting on its end with the lid half-open.

"Well done, thou sharp-eyed Indian maiden!" cried Gerald. "Fetch it then—we're going to be late for breakfast."

Philippa set off on a roundabout route in order to avoid the rock-pools, across the cove towards the picnic hamper. Had she completed the journey she would surely have discovered the tiny person stretched out, unconscious, on the sand—

even though the figure was no bigger than her favourite doll from her dolls' house! The little woman, who was no more than fifteen centimetres long, was wearing a tattered sailor's uniform and was partly hidden in the shadow of the picnic hamper.

But Gerald called out to his sister before she arrived at the basket. "Phil! *Philippa!*"

Philippa, who was within a couple of metres of the hamper, turned at the sound of her brother's voice.

"Look!" he continued. "Out there!"

Gerald was pointing out to sea. Philippa screwed up her eyes and squinted in the early morning sunlight.

"Where? I can't see anything."

"Yes, you can, you silly goose! Stuck out on that rock! It looks like a sort of . . . sort of model ship . . . except it's bigger than any model I've ever seen."

But the sunbeams were striking straight off the calm waters into Philippa's eyes. "I *still* can't see anything!" she called.

"I'm going out to have a look!" cried Gerald.

The boy sat down to unfasten his boots while his sister, forgetting the picnic hamper for the moment, scampered back across the sand to join him.

Now she could see the ship. And, as her eyes grew accustomed to the sunlight, the tiny vessel became clearer. It certainly looked like some kind of model about two metres in length and it lay within wading distance of the shore. The ship was perfect in every detail with three tall masts and the tattered remains of sails fluttering on each one of them. But it seemed to have suffered some kind of disaster for its bows were lifted out of the water and lodged on a jagged rock.

"It was probably wrecked in last night's storm," Philippa thought. But then, she wondered, who would be foolish enough to attempt to sail such a grand vessel in the previous night's bad weather? And what could have happened to the owner?

Gerald had taken off his boots and stockings and was rolling up his trouser-legs.

"What about breakfast?" asked Philippa.

"We'll just have to be late for breakfast." Gerald shrugged and got to his feet. "At least we've found the picnic hamper. That'll be some sort of excuse." He tested a toe in the sea and then pointed at the wrecked vessel. "I'm not going to leave it out there for anyone to come along and steal," he said.

"It isn't yours to steal either," Philippa pointed out. "You don't know who it might belong to."

"Yes, I do. It's mine. It's treasure-trove. It's finders-keepers." And so saying, he set off to wade out to the wreck, watched by his sister.

Across the empty cove, behind the children's backs, another tiny figure, also dressed in seaman's tattered clothing, was peering across at them from behind the lid of the upturned picnic hamper.

This second little sailor was a man. He was thin and, judging by the way that he was hopping agitatedly from one foot to the other, was of a nervous disposition. His agitation increased as he glanced back inside the hamper where yet another figure lay, unconscious. The third of the trio, also a man, was short and fat and, like his two companions, dressed in sailor's costume.

The thin one ran into the hamper, knelt down and, taking a grip on the fat one's shoulder, shook him roughly.

"Spelbush! Spelbush, wake up!" gulped the thin one, glancing anxiously over his shoulder. "You were right, Spelbush! You *must* wake up! Brelca was wrong! We're here. We've arrived. And they *do* exist. There are such things as giants, Spelbush. Big ones! There are two of them here now, just across the beach. They're even bigger than we imagined, Spelbush! *Please* wake up!"

Then, getting no response from the unconscious figure inside the hamper, the thin one scuttled across the sand to where the female figure lay. "Brelca! Wake up, Brelca!" he stuttered, shaking the woman by the shoulder, exactly as he had shaken the little fat man. "You were wrong! Spelbush was right! They *do* exist. The Gulliver charts weren't fakes at all. They were *real*! We're here, Brelca. We've arrived. Only *do* wake up now—*please*!"

But the unconscious woman did not stir and the little man ran round and round in circles with his head in his hands, frequently glancing across at Gerald who was still wading out to the ship.

"Brelca, oh *please* wake up! You *must*!" he said, urgently, shaking the unconscious form yet again. "They've found the *Antelope*."

"Where are we, Fistram? What is this land?"

The voice came from behind him and the thin little fellow, whose name it seemed was Fistram, looked round, joyfully,

20

at his companion in the hamper who had regained consciousness and was leaning against the half-open lid.

"We're *here*, Spelbush! Look!" And he pointed across the beach at Gerald who, with the water now lapping around his thighs, was covering the last few metres to the ship. "It's the Land of the Giants—Quinbus Flestrinia."

The one called Spelbush frowned and gazed all around the cove. "What's happened to the rest of the ship's company?" he asked.

"Drowned, Spelbush." Fistram shook his head, solemnly. "All drowned—save for you and Brelca and myself." And his expression changed to one of fear and sadness as he added: "What are we going to do?"

But Spelbush seemed not to share his companion's misgivings. Fully recovered now, he unwound what appeared to be a cummerbund from around his waist and shook it out. It proved to be a colourful, ornately decorated flag which he held up importantly, striking a pose.

"I, Spelbush Frelock, master navigator," he began, "do hereby claim this land and all of its dominions, by right of conquest, in the name of his most mighty majesty, Emperor Golbasto Momaren Evlame Gurdilo Shefin Mully Ully Gue the Seventeenth, Monarch of all Monarchs—"

"Not now, Spelbush," broke in Fistram, but the little sailor was in full flow.

"—Monarch of all Monarchs, taller than the sons of men, whose head strikes against the sun, at whose nod the princes of the earth shake their knees—"

"*Later*, Spelbush!" insisted Fistram, interrupting for a

second time. "First things first!"

"I am dealing with first things first," snapped Spelbush, glancing across at Fistram disapprovingly. "We were all agreed that claiming sovereignty would be our first task upon landing." And he struck his pose with the standard once again and continued his declaration: "—whose head strikes against the sun, at whose nod, *etcetera etcetera*—"

"While you stand there *etcetera etcetering*, *I*'m lying here completely at the mercy of those giants!" This time it was the female sailor who had interrupted, having regained consciousness, opened one eye, and who was now glaring at Spelbush balefully.

"Brelca's right, Spelbush," said Fistram, nodding quickly. "They've already found the *Antelope*. Supposing they start to look for us? Wouldn't it be wiser for us to hide now, and claim sovereignty by right of conquest after they have gone away?"

Spelbush considered the suggestion carefully and then folded up his flag. "Oh, very well . . ." he said. "Give me your hand, Brelca."

Together with Fistram, Spelbush helped Brelca to her feet and the three of them looked around for a hiding-place.

Some distance away, Gerald stood thigh-deep in the sea, examining the wrecked vessel.

"It's amazing, Phil!" he called across to his sister. "It's got everything! Every little detail! Portholes; hatches; rigging—and it all *works*—almost as if it was *real*." He paused to take in the name which was painted along the prow of the ship. "That's odd," he said, half to himself. "It's called the *Antelope*."

But if Philippa had heard this last remark of her brother's, she failed to recognize the significance of his words.

"Do hurry, Gerald!" she shouted back to him, impatiently. "We'll be *hours* late for breakfast! Grandfather must be wondering what's happened to us."

Gerald tugged at the ship with both hands, freeing it from the rock on which it had foundered. The vessel floated freely but was listing heavily to one side.

"I shan't be long!" he shouted to his sister. "I'm going to tow her in!"

He unfastened his tie, attached one end of it to the ship's prow and slowly began to wade back to the shore, pulling the vessel behind him.

Over on the beach, the three little people had taken refuge inside the picnic hamper. Fistram's eyes widened with anger as he watched events through a gap in the wickerwork.

"He's pinched our ship!" cried the little man. "The giant's pinched our boat!"

"It's piracy!" stormed Spelbush pompously, joining Fistram by the hole in the hamper. "It's downright international high seas piracy!"

Brelca, the third member of the ship's company, was concerned with a more immediate pressing matter. "I've got a hole in my stocking," she moaned.

Gerald, unaware of the distress he was causing the vessel's crew-members, paused as he heard an ominous gurgling sound behind his back. He turned and, to his horror, watched the good ship *Antelope* keel over slowly on to her side and then, with a last despairing rush of bubbles, sink into the clear blue water and finally come to rest on the sand below. Gerald stared down at the vessel knowing that it was far too heavy for him to lift by himself.

But the boy's dismay was nothing compared with that of the three hidden watchers in the picnic hamper on the shore.

"She's gone!" wailed Fistram. "He's sunk her, Spelbush! The giant's sunk the *Antelope!*"

"I can see that," snorted Spelbush. "It's an outright act of maritime aggression!"

"Every stitch of clothing I possessed was on that ship," moaned Brelca, "apart from these rags I'm standing in!"

Spelbush's anger rose. "In the name of his most mighty majesty, Emperor Golbasto Momaren Evlame Gurdilo Shefin Mully Ully Gue the Seventeenth—" he spluttered.

"Oh, do shut up, Spelbush," said Fistram. "We've got more important things to think about."

"More important? The *Antelope* was a vessel from his majesty's personal fleet—his pride and joy—she was named after the craft in which Gulliver made his momentous voyage to our shores—I trust you realize the full implications of the giant's foul despicable act?"

"Yes," said Fistram gloomily, "it means we can't sail home again."

"It means that I haven't got a thing to wear," said Brelca, equally downcast.

"It means," said Spelbush, pulling himself up to his full tiny height, " . . . it means that we're in a state of *war!*"

Across the beach, watched by his sister, Gerald Garstanton dried his feet on his handkerchief and rubbed the loose

24

grains of sand from between his toes. "We'll probably be able to refloat her at low tide, Philippa," he said, slipping on one of his stockings. "We'll come back down here after breakfast."

"If there *is* any breakfast," his sister replied ruefully, glancing across at the sea-front wall where the morning's holiday-makers were already beginning to assemble, taking their morning stroll along the promenade. "I'll fetch the hamper."

Philippa set off at a run across the beach and the three little people hidden in the picnic hamper exchanged fearful glances at her approach. They drew back into the furthest shadows of the wickerwork as the girl lifted up the basket. But she closed the lid and fastened the strap without looking inside. The three tiny travellers breathed again. For the moment, at least, their presence had gone undiscovered.

Gerald tied his boots, stood up, and waved across at his sister. "Race you to the promenade steps, Phil!" he called.

Philippa nodded and, holding the hamper in one hand by its handle, she set off at a run across the cove. Inside the hamper, the little people clung to the wickerwork, grimly, for dear life, as they were swung violently to and fro.

Back at 14 Khartoum Gardens, Mr Garstanton drummed his fingers on the breakfast-table impatiently. He took his hunter-watch out of his waistcoat pocket, glanced at the time and frowned. "I'm extremely sorry, Miss Mincing," he said to the black-clad boarding-house proprietress who was hovering at his side, "I'm afraid I haven't the faintest idea what could have happened to my grandchildren."

25

Sarah Mincing clasped her hands across her stomach and pursed her lips. "It is now seventeen minutes past nine o'clock, Mr Garstanton," she announced, coldly. "Breakfast in this establishment finishes at quarter past that hour. It always has done and—as long as I am mistress here—it will continue to do so. I shall tell the maid to serve yours now; I cannot delay the meal any longer. I am afraid that the children must forfeit theirs. No matter. Perhaps it will teach them something about punctuality."

"I'm sure, if you would just give them a few more minutes, Miss Mincing—"

"I'm sorry, Mr Garstanton," she replied, smiling grimly. "But the rules *are* displayed for all to see in every bedroom. If they are not to be obeyed, what is the use in putting them there?"

Then, pausing only to cast a disapproving glance at the camera and tripod which the children's grandfather had set up, opposite himself, on the other side of the table, Miss Mincing swept out of the room with a rustle of her stiff black dress.

Seconds later, Millie entered at a dash carrying a single breakfast on a tray. Giving the camera and tripod a wide berth, she scuttled across and bobbed a quick curtsy at Mr Garstanton.

"Y'r breakfast, sir, if you please, sir," she mumbled, sliding the plate in front of him. Then, bobbing another brief curtsy, she scurried out of the dining-room as quickly as she had entered it.

Mr Garstanton looked across at his camera and sighed. He

had intended to photograph the children at breakfast. It would have provided a photographic item to add to the photogravure seaside set: *Picture-postcard No. 5—Breakfast at the Lodgings*. Ah well, the photographic study would have to wait. He tucked into his breakfast of cold bacon and congealed egg without much enthusiasm.

When Gerald and Philippa arrived back at the boarding-house, their grandfather's stick was absent from the elephant's-foot umbrella stand. Neither were his overcoat and panama hat in their usual places on the oriental bamboo hat stand.

Philippa went to put the picnic hamper on the hall table but Miss Mincing appeared at the door to the parlour before it was barely out of her hand.

"In this establishment, little girl, we take things back to where they came from—we don't clutter up the hall with things that don't belong to us."

"Sorry, Miss Mincing," said Philippa meekly. Picking up the hamper again, she followed her brother down the hall and into the dining-room. The old gentleman, they discovered, wasn't in the dining-room either.

"You'll cop it, you will, you two!" grinned Millie, cheerfully. She was hard at work blackleading the dining-room fireplace.

"Cop what?" asked Gerald.

"What for?" asked Philippa.

"Why, cop a load of trouble, that's what! For missing your breakfasts."

The children shrugged.

"Where's Grandfather?" asked Philippa.

"Gone for a stroll. As far as the shops. For some of them there photographical things. And you ain't to lay a finger on that there neither," she said, nodding at the camera and tripod. "It's been left set up on purpose, special." With which, she loaded the blacklead and polishing rags and brushes into her basket, got up from her knees and shot out into the kitchen.

"Come on," said Gerald to his sister. "I'm sure we can scrounge some toast at least."

Leaving the picnic hamper on their usual table, Philippa followed Gerald into the kitchen.

Inside the hamper, still clinging desperately to the wicker-work sides, the three little travellers were recovering from the buffeting they had suffered on the way back from the sea-front. Fistram, the first to regain his equilibrium, peered out through the narrow spy-hole in the hamper across a vast expanse of tablecloth.

"It's all white!" he gasped. "As far as the eye can see—a great snowy wasteland!"

Brelca glanced down at what she was wearing. "I can't go out in winter dressed like this!" she wailed.

"It *can't* be snow—it isn't cold enough," said Spelbush, pushing his companion aside and taking his place at the peep-hole. "It's a tablecloth, you simpleton," he snapped, his eyes becoming accustomed to the outside light.

"A tablecloth?" frowned Brelca. "I'm hardly dressed for dinner either!"

"For all *you* know," said Fistram, "we *are* the dinner."

"You don't mean . . ." began Brelca, fearfully.

"No, of course he doesn't!" said Spelbush. "Do shut up, Fistram, and give me a hand. The sooner we're out of here the better."

Up above his head, Spelbush had spotted a wider gap between the close-knit wicker strands. With Fistram on all fours, Spelbush was able to clamber on to his companion's arched back and examine this larger aperture more closely.

The hole, he discovered, was one that had been put there in the manufacture and formed the section of the hamper where the leather strap which held down the lid was secured. Spelbush took his dagger out of his belt and, still standing on Fistram's back, put his hand through the hole and began to saw at the strap. The leather was thick and old and tough, but Spelbush's blade was sharp and it was not long before he began to make headway.

Gerald and Philippa, perched on stools in the warmth of the kitchen, swung their legs under the table and munched hot buttered toast as they watched while Millie baited a mouse-trap.

"Is it a big mouse, Millie?" asked Philippa. "Have you seen it?"

"Big enough," replied the housemaid, nodding her head vigorously. "I've seen 'is nose and whiskers peeping out, I 'ave, from that there cupboard under the sink."

"Perhaps it's a rat," suggested Gerald, winking at his sister.

"'Tain't no such thing!" said Millie with a shudder. "I

'opes I knows enough to recognize a mousey when I sees one! You mind your business, Master Gerald, and eat that toast up quick afore Ma Mincing takes it into 'er 'ead to poke *'er* nose in. She won't take too kindly to you two being in 'ere, that's something else I knows."

Back in the dining-room, Spelbush had managed to sever completely the strap that held down the lid of the hamper. Now, in turn, the three little people clambered up the inside of the hamper, squeezed through the lid and then lowered themselves, via a mustard-pot, on to the table-cloth.

Fistram and Brelca stood, hands on hips and open-mouthed, gazing around at the vast area of the dining-room, the ceiling that towered high above them, and the enormous pieces of structured furniture on every side.

Spelbush, meanwhile, unwound his cummerbund-flag from around his waist, shook it out a second time, and struck a familiar pose.

"I, Spelbush Frelock," he began, pompously, "discoverer, adventurer and master mariner, do hereby claim this edifice and all that is situate inside it, by right of exploration and in the name of his most mighty—"

"Ssshhh!" hissed Brelca, swinging round on Spelbush and silencing him angrily.

"Not now, Spelbush," put in Fistram. "There isn't *time* for that kind of thing. We must find a way down from here before the giants return."

The three travellers scurried hither and thither across the broad expanse of tablecloth in search of a way down to the floor. It was Spelbush who came across the only means of escape.

"Brelca! Fistram!" he called. "Come here—quickly!"

Mr Garstanton, before going out, had left the exposure bulb, attached by its long thin tube to the camera on the tripod, on the edge of the table. It would be possible—dangerous but certainly possible—to take hold of the bulb, leap out into space, and swing down to the floor below.

"It'll get one of us down," said Spelbush. "And whoever goes can look for some way of rescuing the two that stay behind."

Fistram and Brelca studied the tube and bulb dubiously, and then peered over the table at the floor which seemed a long, long way away.

"Good luck, Spelbush," said Fistram.

"I'd go like a shot," said Brelca, "if I'd anything decent to wear."

"Cowards," snapped Spelbush, dismissing his companions with a scornful glance. Then, wrapping his arms tightly around the exposure bulb, he launched himself off the edge of the table.

It was this action that must have set off the camera's exposure mechanism, for there was an immediate whirring sound from within the polished wooden case. Fistram and Brelca turned at the unexpected sound and stood stock-still, staring into the lens. Then, as Spelbush's feet finally touched the floor, the time-exposure mechanism cut itself out and the whirring sound stopped. Fistram and Brelca exchanged a puzzled glance. Then, leaning over the table's edge, they

31

looked down at Spelbush standing on the floor.

"See if you can find some food!" called Fistram.

"Don't forget to look for something I can *wear*!" shouted Brelca.

Spelbush waved back at them as a sign that he had heard, and then set out on his exploratory quest across the dining-room. He had gone no more than half-a-dozen paces when the kitchen door swung open suddenly and Millie came in with an empty tray.

Brelca and Fistram ran around in circles on the tablecloth while Spelbush scuttled across the carpet and sought refuge under the sideboard.

But the housemaid had noticed none of this. She had paused with one hand on the door to call back to the children in the kitchen. "I'd make myself scarce, if I was you," the housemaid advised them. "I've told you once already—you won't 'arf cop it and no mistake if old Ma Mincing catches you in there!" With which, she turned and crossed towards the table.

The brief respite had given Fistram and Brelca time to run back, up on to the mustard-pot, and then under the lid and once more into the hamper.

"Well, I'm blessed!" gasped Millie, picking up the hamper. "What's all this!"

"What's all what?" asked Gerald who, together with his sister, had taken Millie's advice and come out of the kitchen.

"Why—this of course!" said the housemaid, holding up the picnic hamper and pointing to the severed strap.

The two little folk hidden inside the hamper stood quite still and held their breaths.

"Don't know," said Gerald, surprised and shaking his head.

"It didn't break itself, I'm sure," said Millie. "It's not even *broken*," she added, giving the strap a closer inspection. "Why—it's been deliberately cut, has that!"

"It *wasn't* us, Millie," repeated Gerald, firmly.

"We didn't do it—honestly!" added Philippa.

Millie studied their wide-eyed upturned faces. "Well, I believes you—but it ain't me you've got to convince, is it? *She*'ll go off 'er chump if she sees it." Millie paused and smiled at the children sympathetically. "I'll tell you what I'll do. I'll 'ide it somewheres out of sight and 'ope as 'ow she don't come across it. Not before you and your grandpa 'ave packed your bags and gone at least. Now—why don't you do what I told you in the first place—make yourselves scarce. Go on now—*scoot!*"

The children scooted.

Millie shook her head and smiled again as the hall door closed behind them. Then, placing the mustard-pot and the picnic hamper on the tray, she carried all three into the kitchen.

As Gerald and Philippa went out through the front door of the boarding-house, they very nearly bumped into their grandfather on his way back from the chemist's shop.

"Hello, strangers!" he greeted them, his arms full of brown-paper packages. "And where were you two when the breakfast gong sounded?"

"We went down to the beach this morning, Grandfather," said Gerald.

"To look for the missing picnic hamper," added Philippa.

"Commendable intention, I suppose," said Mr Garstanton, with a nod. "Fruitful journey, was it?"

"Yes," said Philippa.

"No!" put in Gerald, quickly, with a warning shake of his head at his sister.

"Yes and no?" queried their grandfather. "What does that mean exactly?"

Philippa, taking her cue from Gerald, smiled at her grandfather with wide-eyed innocence. "I mean we *thought* we'd found it—but it turned out to be something else."

"Ah!" said the old photographer, nodding understandingly. "I often think I've found the answer to my money problems—but then something turns up to prove me wrong." He frowned, lost in his own thoughts for the moment, tugged at his side-whiskers and then looked down at his grandchildren in surprise, as if he'd almost forgotten they were there. "It's not been much of a holiday for you two, has it?"

"Yes, it has!" said Gerald, loyally.

"We've had a *lovely* time!" agreed Philippa.

"Go on, off you go now and enjoy yourselves," said their grandfather, softly.

The children required no second bidding. They sped off along the street in the direction of the beach.

"And try and get back in time for luncheon!" their grandfather called after them.

But Gerald and Philippa were already out of earshot.

In the kitchen, Millie clambered up on to a stool and lifted the picnic hamper into the shadows on the highest shelf where, she hoped, it would lie unnoticed for several days at least. That done, Millie climbed down from the stool, picked up her basket of blacklead cleaning things and went off about her daily tasks.

A moment later, the lid of the picnic hamper rose slightly and Fistram's head appeared. He glanced down at the kitchen floor which seemed a million miles away. They were trapped on the topmost shelf with no way down.

"It's no good," he sighed to Brelca as he slid back inside the hamper. "We're cut off completely—marooned."

"What do we do next?"

"There's nothing we *can* do, except wait," replied Fistram glumly, "and hope that Spelbush rescues us."

3

Gerald and Philippa blinked as they peered across the wide expanse of shimmering golden sand. Their spirits sank. The wrecked vessel they had left under shallow water before breakfast had disappeared. All that remained on the beach were some splintered pieces of planking. The good ship *Antelope* had been broken up by the outgoing tide.

Leaving his sister behind, Gerald ran across the beach to where the pieces of wreckage lay. He picked up one of the bits of wood and turned it over in his hands. It had come, he realized, from the prow of the ship and the ship's name was clearly visible in flowing white letters: *Antelope*. Gerald frowned, thoughtfully, as the name again stirred something at the back of his mind.

At that same moment, back in the dark of the boarding-house cellar, the children's grandfather also frowned, deep in thought, as he stared at the image that presented itself on one of the photographic plates he had just developed.

The photograph showed two miniature people, a man and a woman, both dressed in tattered sailors' clothing, both fully grown but neither more than fifteen centimetres tall, it seemed, in relation to the table-top on which they were standing and compared with the pepper-pot and salt-cellar at their side.

The old photographer pulled at his side-whiskers as he gazed at the improbable picture.

Later, when his grandchildren had returned, sadly, from the beach, the old man showed them the photograph. The children, like their grandfather, stared at the little people in astonishment.

"Are they *real*?" asked Gerald, wide-eyed.

"They must be dolls," said his sister, equally amazed. "But aren't they lifelike?"

"I'm blessed if I know *who* they are—or where they come from," confessed their grandfather, scratching at his whiskers yet again. "And I'll tell you something else that's got me up a gum-tree . . ." He paused and a knowing smile flickered across his face. ". . . Who put you pair of imps up to it?"

"Put us up to what?" asked Gerald.

"We don't know anything about it," said Philippa.

"No? You didn't, I don't suppose by any chance, study that article in my Summer Number of *The Photographic Camera*?"

"Which article?" said Gerald.

"What about?" asked his sister.

"I may be a trifle muddle-headed, but I'm not *that* much of a muggins," said their grandfather. "Come on. Own up. When did you young imps decide to pull my leg?"

"But we didn't!" The children's voices rang out as one.

"It had to be somebody in this establishment. I doubt that

37

Miss Mincing's the one for playing pranks. And I hardly think that trick-photography is Millie's forte."

"What's trick photography?" asked Gerald.

"I've never even *heard* of it!" wailed Philippa.

"Come off it, you two!" said Grandfather Garstanton with a chuckle. "I forgive you—this time. But who on earth did you get to dress up as sailors and where the dickens did you get those fancy-dress costumes from?"

The children exchanged another puzzled glance and shrugged their shoulders at each other. But, thankfully, before their grandfather could press them further, the luncheon gong rang out from the hall.

"Hullo! Is that the time!" exclaimed Grandfather Garstanton, tugging his watch from his waistcoat pocket and flicking it open. "Lunch already? Shall we pursue this matter later?" And, so saying, he led the way into the hall.

Gerald and Philippa exchanged another glance. This time it was one of relief. Their grandfather, as he himself was the first to admit, did tend towards absent-mindedness. Perhaps, before lunch was over, he'd forget the curious photograph. They, certainly, had nothing they could add to clear up the mystery.

Miss Mincing glanced up from giving the gong another beating. "Only two for lunch today, Mr Garstanton?" she said, pursing her lips.

The old photographer glanced round and discovered that only one of his grandchildren, Philippa, had followed him out into the hall. "On parade, Gerald!" he called back into the parlour.

Gerald was still puzzling over the sepia photograph.

"Coming, Grandfather!" he called, laying the picture of the little people aside. He left the parlour and followed his grandfather and sister into the dining-room. But there was still something nagging away at the corners of his mind.

That night, when the rest of the household was fast asleep, Gerald lay awake in the big brass bed he shared with his sister at the top of the house, staring at the ceiling. An oil-lamp flickered feebly at his bedside. He glanced across at the apparently sleeping figure of Philippa and then drew out the sepia photograph from under his pillow. He leaned across, cautiously, and turned up the oil-lamp slightly. He stared at the photograph for several seconds and then, slowly, slid his feet from under the bedclothes and lowered them to the floorboards.

Ever so carefully, he picked up the oil-lamp and tiptoed towards the door.

"Where are you going?" asked Philippa, sitting upright in the bed.

"Go back to sleep."

"I *wasn't* asleep."

"Then go to sleep now."

"No. I'm coming with you," announced Philippa, already with one foot on the floor.

The orange glow of the oil-lamp cast a circle of light around them as they made their way down the dark-wood staircase of the silent, sleeping boarding-house towards the ground floor. Stuffed birds and animals peered out at them from glass cases, their luminous eyes twinkling, eerily, in the shadows.

Gerald, holding the lamp high, led the way into the parlour where he nodded towards the sofa.

"Sit down."

Philippa obeyed meekly. Gerald placed the oil-lamp on a polished side-table and moved to the bookcase where he ran his finger along one of the shelves.

"What are you looking for?" asked Philippa.

Her brother did not answer. Finding the book he had been seeking, he took it down from the shelf, crossed to his sister's side, sat down, and flicked through the opening pages.

"Listen to this," he said, and then began to read aloud: "*I removed from the Old Jury to Fetter Lane, and from thence to Wapping, hoping to get business among the sailors; but it would not turn to account—*"

"You read that to me yesterday," interrupted Philippa. "It's *Gulliver's Travels*."

"Ssshhh! Listen!" snapped Gerald, returning to his place on the page. "*After three years expectation that things would mend, I accepted an advantageous offer from Captain William Prichard, master of the 'Antelope', who was making a voyage to the South Sea. We set sail from Bristol on May the fourth, sixteen-ninety-nine . . .*" Then, snapping shut the book, Gerald turned and stared solemnly into his sister's eyes. "Well?" he said.

"Well what?"

"It was the *Antelope*! The ship we found this morning in the cove—she was the *Antelope* too. I told you it was too real to be a model. *And* there's the year as well."

"Which year?" Philippa, not understanding, frowned at her brother.

"Sixteen-ninety-nine, you goose! What year is this?"

"Eighteen-ninety-nine."

"You see! Two hundred years exactly."

But Philippa didn't see. "I *still* don't understand what you're talking about," she said.

"*And* there's the photograph as well." Gerald spoke hurriedly, the words tumbling from his mouth. "The little people on the table-top. It *wasn't* trick photography at all."

"How do you mean? How do *you* know what it was?"

"Because I *do* know! Grandfather was right about one thing though: if it *had* been trick photography, it had to be either you or me. Did *you* take that photograph?"

"Of course not! I wouldn't know how."

"And neither would I." Gerald paused and glanced around into the dark shadows that surrounded them on every side. He shivered slightly with excitement. "They're *real*, Philippa. Those little people. They've come all the way from Lilliput—and they're *here*! They're somewhere in this house. *Now.*"

Philippa's eyes widened as she followed her brother's glance around the room. Part of her wanted to believe his words; but another part of her was afraid—although she wasn't quite sure of what.

"Don't be stupid," she said, her voice hardly raised above a whisper. "They *can't* be real."

"It's true." Gerald nodded firmly. "*And* what about the

strap on the picnic hamper? Don't you see, Phil? We *brought* them here. Somehow, they'd got shut inside that hamper. And it was them that cut the strap in order to escape. I'll show you."

Gerald rose, picked up the lamp, beckoned to his sister to follow him, and led the way into the kitchen.

It was Philippa who spotted the hamper.

"Up there!" she said, pointing to the darkness of the top shelf.

Gerald, having placed the oil-lamp on the kitchen-table, climbed up on to a stool and, standing on tiptoe, just managed to lift down the hamper. He handed it, gently, to his sister who put it on the table.

While Gerald was still clambering down from the stool, Philippa opened the lid of the hamper slightly, and looked inside.

Two terrified faces stared back at her, mouths open in amazement.

She slammed down the lid and swallowed, hard.

"They're still inside," she gulped.

Gerald and Philippa held each other's glance across the well-scrubbed top of the kitchen-table, breathlessly. Gerald licked his tongue around the inside of his mouth which had suddenly gone dry.

"Who are you?" he whispered, putting his face close to the hamper.

"Who . . . Who are *you*?" stuttered Fistram.

The two Lilliputians cowered against the side of the hamper as the lid opened again and a huge eye stared in at them.

"Let us out!" demanded Fistram, summoning all his courage. "We demand to see your emperor! We also insist upon our rights according to the Blefuscu Convention! You can't keep us shut up in here—!" But the little man fell silent as, again, the darkness closed in.

Gerald, who had put down the lid, chewed at his lower lip and thought hard.

"Are you going to let them out?" asked Philippa.

Gerald, arriving at a decision, shook his head.

Inside the hamper, the two little people shouted through the wickerwork.

"At least give us some food!" called Fistram. "We haven't had a thing to eat all day!"

"And some clean clothes!" cried Brelca. "We're shipwrecked mariners! We're entitled to a change of clothes! We're entitled to a complete new wardrobe!"

Philippa grinned across at Gerald. "One of them's a girl!" she said, gleefully. "I could make her some clothes. I could dress her up!"

"And what's happened to Spelbush?" Fistram's voice floated out. "What have you done with Spelbush?"

"What on earth is Spelbush?" whispered Philippa, puzzled.

"Someone's name," said Gerald, lowering his voice. "There must be another of them." His eyes roamed the room with all the eagerness of an avid butterfly collector. Aloud, he added: "See if you can find them something to eat, Philippa."

"I do wish we had them back at home, Gerald!" said

43

Philippa, who could hardly contain her joy. It was like the beginning of a grand new game. "They could live in my dolls' house and eat and drink out of my dolls' tea-things!"

Gerald frowned at his sister, warning her to curb her enthusiasm—for the time being at least. He lowered his voice again. "Keep an eye open for the third one," he said.

Philippa nodded and began to search the kitchen for food for the prisoners.

Gerald placed his mouth close to the hamper once again. "Who's Spelbush?" he asked. "What happened to him? Where did he go?"

Inside the hamper, Fistram and Brelca smiled with relief. The giants hadn't managed to catch Spelbush then. Their companion was still free. And as long as Spelbush was at large, there was hope for them.

"You won't catch Spelbush!" boasted Fistram, through the wickerwork. "He's far too cunning for you!"

"He'll have us out of here in no time," added Brelca.

Out in the kitchen, Philippa held up a small wooden barrel she had found. "It's full of biscuits," she announced. "Do you think they'd like them broken up? Broken biscuits are always very popular at my dolls' tea—" She broke off at the sound of a tiny voice that seemed to be coming from somewhere near her feet.

"Help!" cried the voice. "Help me! Help me, please!"

Philippa beckoned to Gerald to join her. He picked up a heavy flat-iron from the fireplace and put it on the hamper lid for safety's sake, then tiptoed to where his sister was standing not far from the kitchen sink.

"Please help me! Here! Down here! Help— *please*!"

The voice was coming, thought Gerald, from inside a cupboard underneath the sink. He knelt down, opened the cupboard door and peered around among the scrubbing-brushes and the floor-cloths.

Suddenly, he laughed out loud.

"What is it?" asked Philippa. "What's so funny?"

"It's Spelbush," said Gerald, lifting up a tiny wriggling figure from whose clothes dangled Millie's mouse-trap. "He's *far* too cunning to be caught by us—but he's not cunning enough to avoid a mouse-trap!"

"Put me down, sirrah!" snapped Spelbush, kicking out in an unsuccessful attempt to free himself from Gerald's grip. "Put me down at once—or you'll suffer for it!" With which, the little fellow pulled out a dagger from his belt and held it, threateningly, over the boy's thumb.

"You do—if you dare!" said Gerald, holding the struggling figure at arm's length above the floor. "One pin-prick and I'll drop you!"

Spelbush glanced down at the floor fearfully, and immediately gave up all physical resistance. Instead, he puffed out his chest, importantly, and tried a different tactic.

"I, Spelbush Frelock, navigator and discoverer, do claim you as my prisoner by right of conquest!"

Gerald grinned and released the mouse-trap from his captive's coat-tail.

"Isn't he a *dear*!" said Philippa. "Do look at his dear little feet! Look at his dear little pink toes—they've all got dear little toe-nails!"

"I am *not* a dear, ma'am," snapped Spelbush huffily. "I am Spelbush Frelock, official emissary of his most mighty majesty, Emperor Golbasto Momaren Evlame Gurdilo Shefin Mully Ully Gue the Seventeenth, and it is my duty to warn you both—"

But Spelbush's words came swiftly to a stop as Gerald opened the lid with his free hand and popped the little sailor into the hamper with his two companions.

"Hello, Spelbush," said Fistram. "Back again?"

Spelbush brushed himself down and smoothed his rumpled clothing in an attempt to regain lost dignity. "If the ship's log ever turns up, Fistram," he said, "you will enter in it that on this day I, Spelbush Frelock, did take as prisoner two of the giant native population—"

And then, for the second time, Spelbush's words were cut short as the hamper was lifted into the air and the three little people grabbed at the sides to keep their balance.

"We'll take them up to our room," said Gerald, who had picked up the hamper. "You get some milk and bring those biscuits."

"Help! Help us!" cried the Lilliputians at the tops of their voices from inside the hamper. "Abduction! Kidnap! *Help us!*"

Gerald glanced around the kitchen and spotted a shawl on a chair by the kitchen range.

"Pass me that, Phil," he said.

Philippa handed the shawl to her brother and he wrapped it around the hamper, muffling the cries.

"Ready?" he said.

46

Philippa nodded.

Gerald picked up the oil-lamp in his free hand and went out through the kitchen door followed by his sister who was carrying the biscuit-barrel and a jug of milk. The journey upstairs was accomplished without further incident—until Philippa stumbled and tripped over the top stair. She managed to keep her balance *and* a tight hold on the milk-jug, but the biscuit-barrel fell on to the uncarpeted landing and the sound echoed round the upper floor. Hastily picking up the biscuit-barrel, she scampered into the bedroom after her brother.

A few moments later, another door opened on the landing and Grandfather Garstanton peered out in nightshirt and nightcap, holding aloft his own oil-lamp. He crossed the landing, opened the door to the children's bedroom and peered inside. They were both lying in bed as quiet as mice.

"Did I hear some sort of a disturbance?"

"Yes, Grandfather," said Gerald, pointing at the jug on the bedside table. "Philippa couldn't sleep so I went down to the kitchen and brought her up a drink."

"Very commendable," said Grandfather Garstanton. "But isn't it about time that lamp was turned out? We're travelling home tomorrow, remember. It's going to be a long and tiring journey."

"Goodnight, Grandfather," said the children in unison.

"Goodnight again. Sleep tight," said the old photographer as he went out, gently closing the door behind him.

Instead of turning out the lamp, Gerald leaned over and looked underneath the bed where the hamper was hidden, its

47

lid securely weighted down. He listened for a moment but there was no sound.

"I think they must have gone to sleep," he said, rolling back into bed.

The two children lay side by side staring up at the flickering shadows cast on the ceiling by the oil-lamp, both lost in their own thoughts.

Underneath the bed, inside the hamper, the little people were far from asleep. They were munching on broken biscuits and passing round the milk—which they drank out of a thimble that had come from Philippa's travelling sewing-box.

As they ate and drank, the Lilliputians held a whispered conference.

"Here's what I propose," said Spelbush. "These two are merely children—"

"Children perhaps," interrupted Fistram, "but they're *enormous*!"

"True, Fistram, but they are still children," continued Spelbush. "And when the time comes for escape, it should prove easier to outwit them than it would the adults of their species. I suggest we go along with the wishes of these children—until it suits us to do otherwise. Agreed?"

Fistram and Brelca exchanged a glance and then nodded their heads.

"Children or no children though," said Brelca, "escape will not be easy."

"I never said that it would," said Spelbush. "But I think that between the three of us we'll find a way."

Above the heads of the three little travellers, in the big brass double bed, Gerald and Philippa were still awake, thinking hard.

"It won't be easy, Phil, if we *do* decide to keep them," whispered Gerald, breaking the silence at last. "They'll take a lot of looking after."

"We looked after that jar of tadpoles last summer," said his sister.

"They'll be *much* more trouble than tadpoles! And they'll have to be kept a secret. No grown-ups must find out about them—or they'd take them away from us. And we'll have to see that they're fed three times a day—"

"And make them clothes," put in Philippa.

"Feed them, clothe them, take them for walks—all kinds of things. It won't be a bit like keeping tadpoles. I just want you to realize, before we take it on, that it isn't going to be easy."

Philippa nodded, solemnly, at the thought of the responsibility and then a smile crept slowly across her face and she hugged herself with joy at the prospect of the days to come.

"It won't be easy—no," she said. "But it will be *fun!*"

With which, she snuggled down happily beneath the bedclothes while her brother leaned across and turned out the lamp.

4

The man who trudged along the sea-shore, carrying a bulging carpet-bag, was tall and thin and unsmiling. He wore a severe black suit with a tightly knotted black tie under his high celluloid collar. His polished black boots reflected the early morning sun. Apparently unaware of the seagulls wheeling and screaming overhead, the man plodded on, absorbed in his own thoughts.

But then he paused as something *did* catch his attention—something bright and shining and half-buried in the wet sand by the water's edge. The man stopped, put down his carpet-bag, stooped and picked up the object. Taking a handkerchief out of a trouser-pocket, he wiped away the loose sand and turned his discovery over in his hand.

He was holding, he realized, a finely detailed small brass bell. There were some tiny letters engraved around the bell and he held it close to his eyes in order to make them out: *Antelope*.

Mildly intrigued with his find, the man slipped the bell into his pocket, picked up his carpet-bag and set off again along the empty beach.

Back at 14 Khartoum Gardens, Millie, the housemaid,

was outside the front door, on her knees with bucket and brush, scrubbing the steps.

It was still very early in the morning and, inside the boarding-house, the Garstanton children were still in bed.

"Gerald? Gerald, are you awake yet?" said Philippa.

"Yes, I've been awake for ages," replied her brother, not looking at her.

"Me too. It really happened, didn't it? All of yesterday? I mean, it wasn't all a dream?"

"No, it wasn't a dream, Phil—it happened right enough. Finding the three little people in the kitchen in the middle of the night—bringing them up here—putting them underneath the bed."

"But are they *still* there?" asked Philippa. "I mean, if it was a *magic* happening, do you think the magic might have worn off now and they've gone?"

Gerald sat up in bed and, turning to look down at his sister, spoke intently. "It wasn't anything magical, Philippa. It was *real*. They came here from far, far away—their boat was wrecked and we found them. Every bit of it was real."

"But are you sure they're still *there*? In the picnic hamper, underneath the bed—have you *looked*?"

Gerald shook his head. "Not yet," he said. "I've been lying here, like you, afraid to look in case they might have gone."

Philippa also sat up and hugged her knees. "I want them to be there so *much*!" she said.

"Let's look now," said Gerald. "Together."

The two children leaned over, one on either side of the

51

bed, and looked underneath it. Their eyes met, upside-down. Yes, the hamper was still there at least. But was there anyone inside it?

Gerald jumped out from underneath the bedclothes, pulled the hamper across the floor and lifted it, gently, up on to the bed. Philippa held her breath as her brother took off the two books that he had placed on the lid the night before to weight it down. Then, slowly, he lifted the lid . . .

Yes! Three small upturned faces gazed back at them.

Gerald quickly slammed the hamper shut.

"They're still there!" breathed Philippa. "Hurrah! What *fun*!"

"Let us out of here!" demanded Spelbush from inside the hamper. "Let us out of here at once!"

Gerald grinned mischievously at his sister who stifled a giggle with her hand.

"I'll let you out," said Gerald, "if you'll cross your heart and promise not to try to escape."

"I am Spelbush Frelock," declaimed Spelbush, through the hamper, in his most important voice, "official emissary to his most mighty majesty, Emperor Golbasto Momaren Gurdilo Shefin Mully Ully Gue the Seventeenth—"

"Isn't he *funny*!" whispered Philippa as Spelbush paused for breath.

"—it is not my policy to cross my heart and enter into promises with small boys!"

"Small!" Philippa mouthed the word, silently, and pointed a finger at the hamper. "Listen who's talking!"

And Gerald was forced to bite his lower lip to stop himself

from laughing out loud. "Stay where you are then!" he said at last, lifting the two heavy books back on top of the hamper. "See if we care!" Then, glancing across at his sister, he went on: "It's time we were getting washed and dressed for breakfast."

Inside the hamper, Fistram and Brelca exchanged a rueful glance while Spelbush folded his arms, proudly, across his chest.

"Oh, *very* diplomatic, Spelbush," said Fistram, bitterly. "Very diplomatic indeed! Well done."

"If you could have done any better, Fistram—"

"He certainly couldn't have done any worse," said Brelca. "I thought it was your idea in the first place to go along with anything they suggest? Let me try and reason with the girl."

"What good would that do?" snapped Spelbush. "She's a child, just like him. We didn't sail across all those stormy oceans, Brelca, to pander to the whims of children who would have us 'cross our hearts'! We came here as adventurers—explorers—*conquerors*!"

"It's rather difficult," sighed Brelca, "to think of oneself as a conqueror from the inside of a picnic hamper!"

"Personally speaking," said Fistram, sadly, "the only thing I feel like conquering right now is a hearty breakfast."

Out on the landing, Grandfather Garstanton knocked on the children's bedroom door and called out to them, "Gerald? Philippa? Are you two up and about yet?"

"Shan't be long, Grandfather!" Gerald called back, hastily pouring cold water from the wash-stand jug into the bowl.

"Almost ready, Grandfather!" added Philippa, dressing quickly.

"Better get a move on, then! Don't forget we've got a train to catch this morning—you haven't even started packing yet!" He took out his watch and studied it. "Five minutes— and I want to see the pair of you downstairs in the dining-room!"

The photographer went on his way down to the hall, where he found himself confronted by the crisp, starched, unsmiling figure of the boarding-house proprietress.

"Good morning, Miss Mincing!"

"Good morning, Mr Garstanton," she replied, her long thin fingers entwined across her black dress. "You'll be requiring your account this morning?"

"Yes, please. Immediately after breakfast, if you would be so kind."

The proprietress watched her guest proceed towards the dining-room and then she herself went into the parlour. Millie, having finished scrubbing the front-door steps some time before, was now on her knees with brushes and black-lead, rubbing hard at the iron fire-grate.

"Goodness, girl!" snapped Miss Mincing. "Haven't you finished that task yet?"

"I've polished the grate in the dining-room, mum, and the ones in the morning-room and front bedroom," said Millie, pushing back her hair with her hand and managing to get a smear of blacklead across her forehead. "I've only this one to finish off and then your room, and the spare bedroom, 'm, and then I'm done."

"And might one enquire, pray, what is happening about breakfast for the guests?"

"Is it breakfast time already, mum?" gasped Millie, who had been hard at work already for two hours that morning.

"Of course it's breakfast time, you silly girl! I don't suppose it's even crossed your mind to simmer the porridge on the hob? Head in the clouds, as usual!"

"Sorry, mum."

"Being sorry doesn't help matters! Now, come along, you good-for-nothing—get a move on!"

Millie gathered together her basket of brushes, dusters and blacklead, clambered to her feet and scurried towards the door. Miss Mincing frowned, sourly, at the fast departing maid-of-all-work and then tested a highly polished table with her forefinger for signs of dust.

The busy housemaid, meanwhile, had scuttled through the dining-room, where she had bobbed a quick curtsied "good morning" to Mr Garstanton who was sitting at his usual table, and then scampered on into the kitchen.

She lifted a huge kettle of boiling water off the kitchen range, poured out a bowlful at the sink, refilled and replaced the kettle, and had just begun to wash the blacklead off her hands when one of the row of bells on the kitchen wall began to jangle. Millie dried her hands hastily, and ran out to answer the bell which was labelled "Front Door".

As Millie ran into the hall, she met Miss Mincing who had just come out of the parlour.

"Where *have* you been, girl?" hissed the boarding-house proprietress. "Never mind, never mind—don't bother to answer—get about your duties. I'll see to the front door."

And, dismissing the maid with a peremptory wave of her hand, Miss Mincing walked down the hall and opened the door.

The man who stood outside was tall, thin, unsmiling and wore a severe black suit and a tightly knotted black tie under a high celluloid collar. He also carried a bulging carpet-bag. It was, in fact, the very same man who had walked along the beach earlier that morning.

"Good morning, Sarah," said the man.

"And only yesterday, I was complimenting myself on my good fortune at not having set eyes on you for months!" replied Miss Mincing, brusquely. "So—the black sheep of the family has been fleeced again, has he?"

"Who told you that?"

"No one. Except that the only time you arrive on my doorstep, Harwell, is on those occasions when yet another of your ill-fated business ventures has failed." Miss Mincing paused, looked her brother up and down, sniffed disapprovingly, and then added: "I doubt you've changed much for the better since the last time you turned up."

"Then that makes two of us, Sarah," snarled Harwell Mincing. "For I perceive that *you* are still as stony-hearted as ever. Well? Will you leave your own brother standing destitute in the street for all the world to scoff at?"

Miss Mincing shook her head slowly, and then opened the door wide enough for her brother to enter.

"Come in," she said, and closed the door behind him as he put his bag down in the hall. "If I'm forced to suffer your presence in the district, Harwell, you're more welcome inside my house than out."

"You *have* changed then, Sarah?" said the man, surprised by his sister's apparent kindly attitude towards him.

"Nay, not at all," replied Miss Mincing. "I'm not allowing you in because of any sisterly regard—it's simply that within my home I can keep a better eye on you and thus sleep easier at night—"

She broke off at the sound of footsteps on the stairs. It was the Garstanton children, scurrying down from their bedroom chattering excitedly.

"What shall we call them, Gerald?" babbled Philippa. "May I choose a name for the girl-sailor?"

"They've got names already," replied Gerald, shaking his head. "Lilliputian names. The fat one's name is Spelbush— he says he was the navigator on the *Antelope*. Then there's Fistram, he—" The boy stopped in mid-sentence as he became aware of Miss Mincing standing in the hall with a tall sinister-looking man dressed in black.

Gerald gulped. The stranger was looking at him keenly, as though he had been listening to every word. He *can't* know what we were talking about though, Gerald tried to reassure himself.

Miss Mincing certainly hadn't overheard the children's conversation. She was wearing her normal everyday frown as she snapped at them: "Walk! Don't run! And watch those boots on my polished hall tiles!"

Gerald and Philippa exchanged a secret grin but cut down their pace and meekly walked across the hall and into the dining-room.

"The boarding-house business seems to be flourishing?" observed Harwell to his sister.

Miss Mincing shook her head. "That pair of brats included, Harwell, I've three visitors in all. The third one is their grandfather. And they're packing up sticks and going home this morning. If it's money you're seeking, brother, there's none of it to spare in this house."

"Did I mention money, Sarah? I'll impose upon you for nothing more than a roof over my head and a seat at your table until I'm back on my feet again."

Sarah Mincing sniffed, disparagingly. "And when's that happy day likely to dawn upon us, I wonder?" she said.

"When fortune presents itself, Sarah, I shall snatch at it. Make no mistake about that. I've known bad times and hard luck, but the two things I've never lacked are a sharp eye for the main chance—" he paused and tapped the side of his nose with his forefinger, "—and a keen pair of nostrils for sniffing out the business opportunity."

"*Business?*" scoffed his sister. "Is that your name for it? The last I heard of you, Harwell, you were parading poor unfortunates around the coast and exhibiting them in sideshows, in front of any person fool enough to pay good money to gawp at them!"

"I was managing a freak-show, sister. As honest a business as any other. Aye, and I'd be managing it still, had not my Bearded Lady fallen head over heels in love with my Wild Man of Borneo."

"And how could that have been of detriment to you?"

"She shaved off her beard for him," growled Harwell. "While he, poor fool, became as docile as a new-born lamb! The pair of them took off together and left me stranded in Rhyl."

"More fool you then," snapped Sarah Mincing, "for allowing them to do it!"

"I'll find something else with which to line my purse, sister—never fear."

"Not in this house, Harwell. That I promise you. There's nothing here that could appeal to your perverse nature."

And so saying, she led the way along the hall. Harwell Mincing picked up his carpet-bag and followed his sister. His shifty eyes darted everywhere, missing nothing and taking in every detail.

Up on the top floor, inside the children's empty bedroom, the lid of the picnic hamper on the bed lifted slightly, moving the two books that were balanced on top. Inside the hamper, Fistram and Brelca braced their legs, planted their hands underneath the lid again, and prepared to push.

"Once more, Brelca," urged Fistram. "We definitely moved it last time."

"Don't just *stand* there, Spelbush—help us!" said Brelca, glancing at the third member of the *Antelope*'s company who was idling against the wickerwork wall.

"Why should I?" said Spelbush, with a lazy shrug of his shoulders. "I thought we were agreed to stay where we were?"

"Spelbush Frelock—adventurer—explorer—conqueror of picnic hampers!" scoffed Fistram.

59

"I mean stay where we are for the time being," replied Spelbush, crossly. "I thought that was the plan?"

"I didn't know that we *had* a plan," said Fistram.

"*I* thought we'd agreed *not* to enter into any agreements with the children?" said Brelca.

"Who said anything about entering into agreements with them?" said Spelbush. "I thought the whole idea was to lull them into a sense of false security—then make good our escape when it best suits our purpose. For the time being, we were going to let them feed us and clothe us."

"*Clothe* us!" gasped Brelca.

"Feed us!" snorted Fistram.

"Look at me!" Brelca continued. "I haven't been offered a stitch of clothing since the shipwreck!"

"Feed us like they did last night?" scoffed Fistram. "Biscuit crumbs and milk? I'd rather take *my* chances out in the giants' world." Then, placing his hands up on the hamper lid again, he turned to Brelca. "Let's give it one more try," he said.

They pushed again, with all their strength, and the lid began to rise, slowly. On top of the lid, the heavy books began to slide towards the bed.

"Push, Brelca!" urged Fistram. "*Harder!*"

As the lid rose the heavy volumes slid over the edge of the hamper, teetered for a second, and then dropped, bouncing off the bed and on to the floor.

"*Crash!*" The books struck the wooden floorboards with such a clatter that the noise resounded through the boarding-house.

Down in the dining-room, where the Garstanton family were still at breakfast, the children's grandfather glanced up at the ceiling as he heard the sound.

"That's odd!" said Mr Garstanton. "I wonder what it was?"

While her grandfather's eyes were directed upwards, Philippa snatched at opportunity, leaned across and stole the last sausage from off his plate, dropping it quickly on to the napkin on her lap. When the old man transferred his eyes from the ceiling back to his plate, he frowned. His memory was not what it had been in his younger days, but he could have sworn that there had been an untouched sausage on his plate a moment before. He glanced across at his grandchildren suspiciously, but they returned his gaze with wide-eyed innocence.

Wondering if, perhaps, the sausage could possibly have rolled off his plate and on to the floor, Mr Garstanton glanced underneath the table. As he did so, Gerald leaned across, stole the last piece of toast from the toast-rack and added it to the sausage on his sister's lap.

The children smiled broadly at each other. The three little people would soon be dining on more than milk and biscuits!

But, unknown to their young captors, the three Lilliputian travellers had escaped from the hamper and were now scampering about the bedclothes, looking for a means of getting down to the floor. At least, *two* of them were scampering about on the bed—the third one was watching his companions, disapprovingly.

"I hope you realize, both of you, that you're undoing all

61

the good work I've achieved," said Spelbush. "I'd just got those children trusting me."

"Yes, Spelbush," said Brelca, pausing for a moment in her mad rush hither and thither, "they trusted you implicitly—that's probably why they kept you locked inside a picnic hamper!"

"Over here, Brelca!" called Fistram, excitedly. "Quick—come and give me a hand!"

He had discovered Gerald's pyjama trousers sticking out from under the bedclothes and was now doing his best to free the pyjama cord. Brelca joined him and they pulled together. Slowly, the cord began to come out.

"You won't even get past the door!" scoffed Spelbush, watching them at their labours. "And even if you did get out on to the landing, have either of you any idea what it's like out there? Where do you think you're going to go?"

"As far away from here as possible," said Brelca.

"There's a cat downstairs, you know," said Spelbush. "An enormous brute like a big hairy elephant! I was hiding from it yesterday when I tangled with that mouse-trap. You won't survive out there! What do you think you can possibly achieve?"

"Breakfast, for a start," said Fistram, yanking free another arm's length of the pyjama cord.

"Cat's breakfast, like as not—and you'll provide it," said Spelbush, darkly.

"I don't *care*," snapped Brelca. "I'm going to go out there and find a change of clothes or die in the attempt!"

"Food! Clothes! Are they the only things that you pair

ever think about?" stormed Spelbush. "It takes *time* to plan an escape. Those children could be our salvation. If it's ever our intention to get back home, they could help us build a boat. If we need to travel across open country, they could carry us further in five minutes than we could cover in a *week*! We *need* their help! Fistram—think about it, that's all I ask. Doesn't anything ever get through to you?"

"Yes, Spelbush," said Fistram. With Brelca's help he had succeeded in freeing the pyjama cord and he was now tying one end of it, securely, to a brass bed-post. "Something's getting through to me at this very moment—up my nostrils—it smells very much like crispy bacon." He tossed the free end of the pyjama cord over the edge of the bed and it hung down as far as the floor. "Ready, Brelca?" he said.

"After you, Fistram."

Then, in turn, the two little people slithered down the pyjama cord, hand over hand, and set off across the floor.

"Fools! Fainthearts!" Spelbush called after them, indignantly. "We sailed across the seas to colonize a kingdom—and all that concerns you two are your stomach and your wardrobe!"

But Fistram and Brelca weren't even listening. They had arrived at the bedroom door which was securely shut. Fistram got down on his hands and knees to peer through the crack between the floor and the bottom of the door. But it was certainly not wide enough for them to crawl through. He clambered back on to his feet and shook his head, sadly. Together they stared up at the door-knob.

"It's hopeless, Brelca. Even if we could get up to it, we

could never turn it."

"Ssshhh!" Brelca placed a forefinger to her lips.

There were sounds of voices from outside.

"Honestly, Grandfather, we can manage our own packing," said Gerald as the three Garstantons mounted the flight of stairs that led up to the top landing.

"We packed our trunk ourselves when we came away," added Philippa.

"And a rare old pig's breakfast you made of it too," chuckled their grandfather.

"That's why we'd like the chance to try again—" Gerald began, earnestly.

"Oh, *please*, Grandfather!" put in Philippa, interrupting her brother.

"—to prove that we can do it properly," ended Gerald.

The two children were desperate, of course, to prevent their grandfather going into the bedroom and discovering the little people. But the old gentleman was not listening. He was looking curiously at Philippa who had both her hands behind her back.

"Philippa, what are you hiding?" he asked.

"Nothing, Grandfather," she replied, meekly.

"Show me your hands."

Philippa, who was holding on tight to the napkin holding the stolen sausage and toast, slipped it into her right hand and kept it hidden behind her back while she withdrew her left hand and extended an open palm. But the old gentleman was not fooled.

"And now the other one," he said.

Philippa slipped her left hand behind her back, swapped the napkin and its contents from right hand into left, and next extended an empty right hand.

"I mean both of them at once, Philippa!" said her grandfather, testily.

Philippa gulped and then, slowly, brought out her right hand.

Surprisingly, it was empty!

"I told you—nothing, Grandfather," she said, and then added, pleadingly: "Mayn't we pack our trunk ourselves? Oh, *please*!"

"I suppose I do have things to do myself," replied Grandfather Garstanton, reluctantly. He felt that he had wrongly accused his granddaughter and that he ought to make amends. "I haven't settled our account yet with Miss Mincing—Oh, very well, then, you can have a shot at packing your trunk at least—"

Before the words were out of his mouth, his grandchildren were scampering towards their bedroom. Philippa, in her excitement, completely forgot about the napkin full of food that she had tucked into the waistband of her frock and which was now suddenly visible to Mr Garstanton.

"Philippa!" he called, sharply.

But he was too late. The bedroom door was already open and the children inside. The old photographer shook his head in mild exasperation, smiled, turned, and set off downstairs again in search of the boarding-house proprietress.

Inside the children's bedroom, Brelca and Fistram had

been waiting by the foot of the door and, as the children rushed in, the tiny pair scuttled out unnoticed.

Gerald and Philippa, who had expected to find their three prisoners still safely held captive in the picnic hamper, came to a sudden horrified stop at the sight of the hamper standing open on the bed. Beside the hamper stood the solitary figure of Spelbush, his arms folded importantly across his puffed-out chest.

"Who let you out?" gasped Gerald. "Where are the other two?"

"Gone," said Spelbush.

"*Gone!*" gasped Philippa. "Gone where? I've been to a great deal of trouble to bring you all some breakfast!"

"It doesn't matter where they've gone," said Spelbush, with a careless shrug of his shoulders. "They are neither of them empowered to enter into diplomatic negotiations. Only myself, Spelbush Frelock, am his most imperial majesty's official emissary. You'll be pleased to hear that I've been giving your proposal for some sort of an agreement serious consideration—"

"Oh, do shut up!" snapped Philippa, cross at the thought that all her efforts had been for nothing.

"Now see here, little girl—"

"Don't you call me *little*!" retorted Philippa, shaking a forefinger at Spelbush. "And stop being so pompous! You've been very naughty. It wasn't easy stealing this breakfast for you!"

"Look, Phil!" cried Gerald. He had been searching the bedclothes and had just discovered the pyjama cord dangling from the brass bed-post. "They must have got down from here—perhaps they're still somewhere in the room."

But the door which he himself had left ajar suggested otherwise.

As her brother ran out on to the landing, Philippa waggled her finger at Spelbush again. "Don't you dare move an inch!" she warned him.

Fistram and Brelca, all this while, had been helping each other down the stairs, step by step. They had arrived on the first floor landing and were just about to set off on their descent of the lower flight of stairs when they heard the children coming.

Gerald and Philippa, working their way slowly down the staircase, were scanning each separate tread in turn.

Fistram and Brelca cowered against the back of the stair on which they were standing and sighed sadly. There wasn't time for them to reach the comparative safety of the hall where there were hiding-places a-plenty. There was to be no escape. It would only be a matter of seconds now before they were discovered . . .

"What on earth do you pair think you're about?"

The voice belonged to the children's grandfather who was standing at the foot of the staircase in the hall, holding a bill that he had just collected from Miss Mincing and gazing up at Gerald and Philippa disapprovingly. "I thought you'd gone off to do your packing?"

The children gazed back at their grandfather guiltily over the banister-rail.

"We . . . We came out to look for something . . ."

stammered Gerald.

"Might one enquire exactly what?"

They glanced at each other, lost for excuses, and then both spoke at once.

"Phil's hair-slide—" said Gerald.

"Gerald's handkerchief—" said Philippa.

"We're not going to miss our train, surely, for the want of a hair-slide *or* a handkerchief?" said Grandfather Garstanton. "Back upstairs the both of you and get on with that packing."

The children hesitated.

"You heard me—*scoot*!"

They scooted.

The old photographer went on his way into the parlour.

Brelca and Fistram grinned at each other with relief and then continued their descent of the staircase.

5

Grandfather Garstanton crossed the plush-curtained aspidistra-dotted parlour and sat down at the writing-desk. He took out his cheque book, picked up the pen and dipped it in the pewter inkpot. He was just about to write out a cheque when something caught his attention.

He picked up the object from the desk and turned it over in his hand. It was a small, finely detailed, brass bell. Intrigued, the old man rang the bell between thumb and forefinger.

"Curious little object, is it not?"

Grandfather Garstanton, surprised to discover that he was not alone in the room, turned in his chair and peered into the shadowy corners where the sunlight was never allowed to penetrate for fear that it might fade the wallpaper.

A tall dark man dressed in black was standing by the bookcase with an open volume in his hand.

"You surprised me, sir," said Mr Garstanton. "I was not aware that there was anyone here apart from myself. Are you a guest here too?"

The dark man shook his head and smiled. "A temporary exile from the world of business," he said, walking across and extending his hand. "Harwell Mincing, sir—at your service."

"Ralph Garstanton, sir—similarly at yours," replied Mr Garstanton, rising to his feet and shaking hands.

"And as to that bell you're holding," said Harwell Mincing, "might one enquire what you make of it exactly?"

"Is it yours, then?" asked the children's grandfather, glancing down again at the bell.

"I came across it this morning on the beach. I'd value your opinion."

Mr Garstanton shook his head and smiled. "I'm a photographer, not an antiquarian," he said.

"All the same, I'd be grateful to hear what you think of it. Is it old?"

"Difficult to tell. It's brass. An intricate little piece. Finely detailed. There's care and craftsmanship gone into the making of it . . ."

"There's an inscription around the rim."

Mr Garstanton peered closely at the bell. "So there is!" he exclaimed. "A–N–T–E–L–O–P–E. *Antelope*. Well, I never! As you observe, Mr Mincing, a curious little object. Though I'd hesitate to place any great value on it."

"And what would you say was its purpose, sir?"

The old man shrugged and shook his head. "Who can tell? At best, an oriental temple decoration—at worst, a cage-bird's plaything. Pray, sir, tell me. What do you yourself make of it?"

Harwell Mincing took the bell from the photographer and slipped it into his jacket pocket. "Are you a literary man, Mr

Garstanton?" he asked, apparently changing the subject.

"No, sir. Not much of one—apart from the perusal of my bi-monthly periodical, *The Photographic Camera.*"

"Are you, perhaps, conversant with this book?" And Harwell Mincing held up the volume he had been reading.

"*Gulliver's Travels*?" Mr Garstanton read the title on the spine of the book. "I believe the children have an edition in the nursery back at home. But I must confess that I've never glanced inside it."

"You should, sir. You should. A vividly written and extremely well-documented journal."

With which, and taking with him both bell and book, Harwell Mincing strode from the room. Had he glanced down as he crossed into the hall, he might well have seen the two little people who had been standing outside the open parlour door. But Harwell was too immersed in his own thoughts to pay any attention to what was going on around him.

Brelca and Fistram, on the other hand, had heard every word of the conversation that had taken place in the parlour.

"That man knows everything," whispered Brelca, solemnly, nodding after the departing figure of Harwell Mincing as he moved off towards the kitchen.

"Nonsense!" replied Fistram. "He knows nothing. He's found the ship's bell, that's all. He's putting two and two together and counting six. He can't know that we're in this house."

"Perhaps not," agreed Brelca. "All the same, we must be

on our guard. If those children were to let slip any untoward remark . . ."

"It's as important to those children, Brelca, as it is to ourselves, that our presence here goes undetected. They won't say a word to anyone."

"I still think it's our duty to tell Spelbush what we've heard."

"You're not suggesting that we . . .?" Fistram looked back at the staircase they had not long before descended. It stretched upwards and away in front of them like some tall, steep mountain. It would be far more difficult to climb up it than it had been to come down. "On an empty stomach?" ended Fistram, sadly.

"We *must*," said Brelca, nodding firmly.

Fistram let out a long-suffering sigh. Brelca was right, of course. It *was* their duty to report back to Spelbush. All the same, it would have been nice to scout around and have some breakfast first. Letting out a second sigh, Fistram crossed to the foot of the towering stairs where he got down on all fours and motioned to Brelca to use his back as a stepping-stone up on to the first tread. Once there, he reckoned, she would be able to give him a hand up and they could then tackle the next tread, and each one after it, in the same way. It was going to be a long, laborious back-aching journey up to the top floor, but Fistram couldn't think of an easier way.

But before Brelca could take advantage of Fistram's offer, they heard a low angry purring sound coming from somewhere over their heads. Looking up, they were horrified to see a huge menacing marmalade tom-cat crouched on the stairwell above them, its claws out, its teeth bared, its diamond green eyes glowering down at them, ready to pounce.

Fistram and Brelca stood stock-still for a split-second, as though mesmerized, gazing up at the terrifying creature.

"Run!" screamed Fistram, finding his voice.

The two little people turned as one and raced across the hall tiles as the boarding-house cat drew back and then launched itself in pursuit.

Fistram and Brelca flung themselves to the floor and rolled under the hall bureau in the nick of time. In one leap, the marmalade cat had arrived on the very spot the two little people had occupied a moment before. Luckily, the gap between the floor and the bottom of the bureau was not wide enough for the cat to crawl underneath. It could do no more than make an exploratory sweep with its paw. Fistram and Brelca, on hands and knees, cowered back as the needle-sharp claws swept past them. There was just enough room to keep out of range of the cat's paw and, for the time being at least, the two little people were safe.

But the marmalade cat was in no hurry and was more than content to enjoy the sport of lying in wait. Settling itself on its haunches by the bureau, ready to pounce and biding its time, the cat purred threateningly and waited for its captives to make a move.

Mr Garstanton, coming out of the parlour carrying in his hand the cheque he had just made out for Sarah Mincing, paused as he saw the cat poised to strike.

"Hello, old fellow," said the photographer. "What have you got trapped underneath there then—is it a mouse?" He was about to stoop and peer under the bureau himself, when the grandfather clock in the hall began striking ten. "Bless my soul!" murmured Mr Garstanton, fishing his watch out of his waistcoat pocket and double-checking the time. "Is it that hour already? . . . I hope you children are packed and ready?" he called up the stairs. "There'll be a hansom cab here in fifteen minutes to take us to the railway station!"

With which, forgetting the cat, he moved on towards the dining-room in search of Miss Mincing as Millie, armed with her basket of brushes and dusters, scuttled past him on her blackleading duties.

Up in the top bedroom, the children's trunk was packed and ready to be taken downstairs. Gerald and Philippa, wearing their outdoor things, were sitting on the edge of the bed in serious conversation with Spelbush.

"I still don't see *why* we can't take him back with us," said Philippa, tearfully, to Gerald.

"I've explained why not, Phil," said Gerald, gently. "It wouldn't be fair."

"Of course it wouldn't, little girl," said Spelbush. "The idea's quite unthinkable."

"We couldn't take him and leave his friends behind," continued Gerald. "That would be cruel."

"But *I* wouldn't be cruel," said Philippa, shaking her head firmly. "I'd be extremely *kind* to him." She turned to Spelbush and continued, coaxingly. "You could live in my dolls' house in the nursery. There's lots of furniture *and* carpets on the floor. You can even draw the curtains. You'd have a *lovely* time."

74

"But he *wouldn't*, Philly, that's just the point," said Gerald. "It'd be like keeping white mice or guinea-pigs. They need to be kept in pairs or else they *die*."

"Not that I *like* being compared with white mice *or* guinea-pigs," said Spelbush, frowning. "But in principle, little girl, your brother is telling the truth."

"All right," said Philippa, turning back to Gerald, "but why can't we look for the others and keep all three?"

"Because there isn't time," replied Gerald. "We wouldn't know where to start—they could be anywhere in the house and we're leaving in a minute."

As if to emphasize Gerald's words, the door opened and the children's grandfather entered from his own room across the landing, his arms loaded with his bags and his photographic paraphernalia.

Philippa, acting quickly, covered Spelbush with her hat.

"Well done, troops!" said Mr Garstanton, beaming as he spotted the waiting trunk. "All packed and ready to move off then, eh? Kitchener would be proud of you. Parade downstairs at the assembly point. Can you manage that trunk between you, or will you need a helping hand?"

"We can manage, Grandfather," said Gerald.

"That's the ticket!" said Mr Garstanton, and he ducked out of the room again banging his camera-tripod legs against the door.

Philippa lifted her hat, revealing Spelbush.

"We've got to go now," said Gerald, picking up the little man in his hand. "Where would you like us to leave you?"

"Somewhere near the kitchen, please. If I know Fistram,

75

that's where I'm most likely to find him."

"Come along then," said Gerald, slipping Spelbush into his pocket and taking hold of one end of the trunk. "Catch hold of that end, Phil," he said.

Grandfather Garstanton was waiting by the open front door as Gerald and Philippa came down the last flight of stairs carrying the trunk between them.

"Fall in outside, the Hussars!" cried the old photographer, cheerily. "Transport's waiting!"

As Mr Garstanton led the way outside, Gerald lifted Spelbush out of his pocket. "I'll leave you here in the hall," he said, and then held the little man up in front of his sister. "Say 'goodbye', Phil—quickly."

"Goodbye, little person," said Philippa. Her lower lip trembled. She was close to tears again.

Spelbush inclined his head, courteously. "Goodbye, little girl," he said. "I was really most grateful to you for the offer of the dolls' house furnished accommodation—perhaps I'll avail myself of it on some future occasion."

"We'll never ever see one another again—*never!*" sobbed Philippa, shaking her head fiercely. And she turned and stumbled along the hall, biting back tears and leaving her brother to bring the trunk alone.

Gerald gently lowered Spelbush to the floor, and extended his smallest finger for the little fellow to shake. "Goodbye, Spelbush Frelock," he said.

"Farewell, young man," replied Spelbush, solemnly. "I appreciate everything that you've done for me."

"And good luck," added Gerald; then, rising, he turned to

76

pick up the trunk.

"Spelbush—look out!" It was Brelca's voice that called out to him.

Spelbush turned. In the twinkling of an eye he took in the scene: Brelca and Fistram staring out at him, horrified, from beneath the giant piece of furniture and, between himself and them, the huge marmalade cat, its back arched, snarling, teeth bared, ready to spring.

"Help me! Help!" yelled Spelbush at the top of his voice.

Gerald spun round, dropping the trunk, and reacted quickly. In one movement, he swooped down and snatched up Spelbush while keeping the cat at bay with his free hand.

"Buck up, young 'un!" said Mr Garstanton who had just come back into the house to see what was keeping his grandson.

Gerald slipped the little man inside his overcoat pocket and turned. "Just coming, Grandfather," he said.

"Rally round the flag, then!" said Mr Garstanton, urgently. "You go out and get into the cab. I'll bring that trunk. We're going to miss the train."

Gerald, left with no choice, walked out of the house with Spelbush as his grandfather stooped to pick up the trunk. The door slammed shut behind Mr Garstanton, leaving an empty silence in the hall.

"What do we do next?" gulped Fistram.

Brelca slowly shook her head.

The boarding-house cat was playing its waiting-game again, poised by the bureau, ready to pounce if they so much as ventured out.

From the road outside they could hear the rattle of the wheels from the hansom cab which was carrying Spelbush out of their lives for ever.

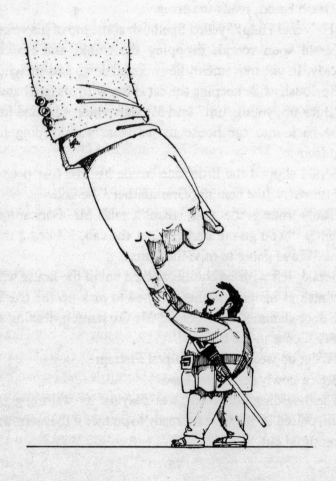

6

"Millie! *Millie!* Do you hear me, girl?" called Sarah Mincing down the stairs from the open door of the bedroom recently vacated by the Garstanton children. "Come up here this instant!"

"Coming, mum!" The housemaid's voice floated up from below.

"The idle good-for-nothing flibbertigibbet!" snapped Sarah, turning back into the bedroom.

"Oh, hang the maid, Sarah," snarled Harwell. "Don't you understand what I'm telling you? They were *here*! In this *house*. In this *room*!"

"Don't talk poppycock, brother!"

"But it's *true*, woman! I only suspected it before but now I'm sure!" Harwell pointed as evidence to the open picnic hamper on the bed and the pyjama cord still dangling from the bed-post. "They were in that very hamper! They climbed down that very cord—" He broke off as his eyes lit up and he bent down to retrieve the tiny shining dagger he had just seen half-hidden between the strands of wickerwork at the bottom of the hamper. "Look at this! *Now* do you believe me! Here's the very knife—their size—they used to cut the hamper-strap!"

It was at this point that Millie arrived upon the scene, breathless, after running up three flights of stairs.

"Yes 'm?" she gasped. "You called me, mum?"

"Never mind 'yes 'm'! I'll give you 'yes 'm', girl! What do you know about this?" said Sarah Mincing, picking up the hamper and holding it up with the broken strap in front of the frightened housemaid's face.

"Nothing, mum—'cepting that it's your picnic 'amper, ain't it?"

"*Was* my picnic hamper, you mean! Until that pair of young hooligans chose to vandalize it! They've cut the strap!"

"The Garstanton children, mum? They wouldn't do that! Never! They was that well-be'aved."

"Well-behaved? Hah!" scoffed Sarah. "Is it good behaviour, in your opinion, to *run* down stair-carpets? Is it good behaviour to cross a well-scrubbed hall in *boots*?"

"They're on'y kiddies, mum. They *be'aves* like kiddies. But that don't mean they'd 'arm things."

"It wasn't those brats that cut the hamper-strap, sister," interrupted Harwell Mincing. "I keep on telling you *they* were inside it."

"*They*? They!" replied Sarah, disparagingly. "*They* don't exist. I tell you, brother, you've spent so much time with your travelling side-shows full of poor unfortunates, you see freaks in front of your eyes wherever you look!"

"These are not freaks, sister!" snapped Harwell. "And I'll not discuss the matter in front of the maid. Curse it, Sarah—

will you argue about a spoiled hamper and let a fortune slip through our fingers?"

"As long as I'm controlling the purse-strings in this household, Harwell—yes!" snapped Sarah. Then, turning back to Millie, she continued: "And I don't blame the hamper on those children, girl—I lay that blame on you."

"Me, mum!" gasped the housemaid. "I don't know nothing about that, mum!"

"Exactly!" announced Miss Mincing, triumphantly. "And thus, girl, by your own lips do you stand condemned! Had you done the work you were set to do this morning, you *would* have known about it. Had you been up to this room earlier, you'd have discovered the hamper and I would have been informed of their mischief before the wicked children left the house. At least I'd have got some recompense."

"I was blackleading all the grates this morning, mum— and scrubbing the front doorstep."

"Excuses, excuses. Always excuses! Thank heaven the holiday season is over at last and I shan't be needing a servant any longer. I was thinking of letting you stay until the end of the month, out of the goodness of my heart—but you can pack your bags today! I've done with you."

"But, mum—"

"Good heavens, girl! Don't waste your last minutes of employment in argument! Will you *never* learn? Get your work completed and pack your things."

"Yes 'm," sighed Millie, and she scuttled from the room.

"A fig for your picnic hamper," snarled Harwell at his

sister. "A veritable fortune has slipped through our fingers—just like that," he added, snapping his fingers. While the conversation had been going on between Sarah and Millie, Harwell had untied the pyjama cord from around the bed-post and examined it closely. Now, tossing the cord on to the bed, he stormed angrily out of the room and down the stairs.

As Harwell crossed the hall, bad-temperedly and without looking where he was going, there was a complaining squeal of pain from beneath his feet. He had inadvertently stepped on the tail of the marmalade cat which was still keeping up its vigil on the bureau.

"Confound the animal!" snapped Harwell.

The cat shot across the hall and vanished into the dining-room, still squealing loudly with pain and anger. As Harwell went on his way into the parlour, Fistram and Brelca crept out from underneath the bureau and stood up, both sighing with relief.

"Well?" said Fistram. "What next?"

"We get out of this house, for a start," replied Brelca. "And our next task then is to find Spelbush."

"Out there?" said Fistram, nodding his head at the front door and indicating the vast world that lay beyond. "It's hopeless—we haven't got a chance."

"We've *got* to find him," said Brelca. "We must formulate a plan."

"And how do you propose we formulate a plan for finding Spelbush when, without Spelbush, we're neither of us any good at formulating plans?"

Brelca, acknowledging the truth in Fistram's words, shook her head, sadly.

Over a mile away, in the otherwise empty waiting-room of the local railway station, Spelbush and Philippa watched as Gerald wrote something in his pocket-book.

"That's the name and address of the place that we've just come from: *Miss Mincing, 14 Khartoum Gardens, off the South Promenade*," said Gerald, tearing out the page and handing it to Spelbush.

"Thank you, young man," said Spelbush, taking the piece of paper. The notebook page was almost as big as the little chap himself and he was forced to hold it at arm's length in order to make out the writing.

"I'll fold it up for you," said Gerald, taking back the piece of paper and folding it into a manageable packet for Spelbush to carry. Spelbush took back the wad of paper and tucked it under his arm.

"I can't imagine how you're ever going to find your way back there," said Philippa in worried tones.

"There's no need to concern yourself on my account, little girl," replied Spelbush, loftily. "I am Spelbush Frelock, master navigator. The very same Spelbush Frelock that charted the *Antelope*'s course around the world. The same Spelbush Frelock that—"

"Yes, yes!" interrupted Gerald. "But there isn't time to go into all that now!"

"In any case, it makes no difference what you've done before—this journey's different. It won't be as if you can stop anyone and ask the way."

"I'll get there," said Spelbush, determinedly.

"It's going to take you days, you know—weeks, perhaps," said Gerald, "and even if you find the house, it's possible your friends will have moved on somewhere else."

"I'll take that chance."

"Are you sure you wouldn't rather stay with us—" began Philippa, but she broke off as the waiting-room door opened suddenly.

"Helloa! And what tricks have you two been getting up to?" said their grandfather, taking in the guilty expressions on the faces of the two children.

"None, Grandfather," said Gerald, hastily concealing Spelbush under his cap.

"Y'know, someone, some day, in the fullness of time, will come up with a railway timetable that's comprehensible to the common man," said the old photographer, changing the subject. "I might even have a shot at it myself. I could have sworn that I was given to understand that there was a train at twenty-three minutes past ten this morning—but according to the station master, there isn't one until twenty-four minutes past eleven."

But Gerald and Philippa weren't listening. Their thoughts were elsewhere. They were worried about Spelbush and the long and hazardous journey that he was about to undertake.

"Cheer up, troops!" said their grandfather, assuming that the children's gloomy expressions were due to the non-arrival of their train. "It's not the end of the world, y'know!" he added, breezily.

"It might not be the end of *your* world, Grandpapa," said Philippa, solemnly, "but it could be the far corners of the earth for someone else."

Grandfather Garstanton blinked as he tried to puzzle out the meaning of his granddaughter's words.

Back at 14 Khartoum Gardens, Millie's few possessions were contained in a sheet-wrapped bundle lying in the hall by the front door.

"There's four shillings and ninepence there, young woman," said Sarah Mincing, coldly, as she counted coins into the housemaid's hand. "Nobody can say I'm not being over-generous—but there you are, that's my nature."

"Thank you, mum," said Millie, bleakly.

"I've paid you right up until lunchtime, which is far more than you deserve. But I've stopped you eightpence half-penny, which is what it's going to cost to get the hamper mended—and three farthings more for squandering black-lead by applying it too thickly."

"Wherever am I to go, mum, at such short notice?"

"Perhaps you should have thought about that, girl, when you were slapping blacklead everywhere as if your mistress was made of it," snapped Sarah Mincing and, putting an end to the conversation, she turned and flounced off down the hall.

Millie picked up her bundle and went out through the front door and down the street, her shoulders drooping sadly.

An hour later, a bright green engine, pulling six gleaming carriages, drew up with a hiss of steam and a squeal of brakes at the station platform. As Gerald, Philippa and their grandfather came out of the station waiting-room, a forlorn figure trudged on to the other end of the platform carrying a sheet-wrapped bundle.

"Look, Grandfather!" exclaimed Philippa, as the porter lifted their luggage into a second-class carriage. "It's Millie—from the boarding-house!"

"Are you *sure*?" said Grandfather Garstanton, peering along the platform.

"It is, Grandpapa! It *is*!" replied Philippa, excitedly.

"I bet that awful Miss Mincing has given her the sack," said Gerald. "She was always threatening that she would."

"Mayn't she come and work for us, Grandfather?" begged Philippa. "You said we'd need to look for a housemaid as soon as we got home."

"How do you know she's got the sa . . . been dismissed?" asked Grandfather Garstanton.

"I'm sure she has," said Philippa. "She looks so sad."

"What else would she be doing at the station?" said Gerald. "And why is she carrying all her things?"

"And even supposing she *has* been dismissed from her post with Miss Mincing," said the children's grandfather, "how do you know she'd *want* to come and work for us?"

"I just *know* she would," said Philippa. "She liked us ever so—*and* we got on with her. Oh, *do* ask her, *please*, Grandfather! *Quickly!* The train will be leaving soon and then it will be too late!"

Mr Garstanton gazed into the upturned, pleading faces of his two grandchildren and then, having made up his mind, walked the length of the platform and spoke to the housemaid.

Gerald, meanwhile, had gone to the rear of the platform and, in the shelter of a hand-truck full of milk-churns, was putting Spelbush on the ground.

"Good luck again," said Gerald, bidding farewell to the little man for the second time that morning.

"Goodbye!" replied Spelbush, taking a firm grip on the folded piece of notepaper.

Gerald got to his feet and, turning his back on Spelbush, moved across the platform to join his sister. Mr Garstanton was walking down the platform towards them accompanied by a beaming Millie.

"Well, now!" said the housemaid. "Isn't this grand then! No sooner out of one job than I'm fixed up with another! A nice spot of luck I calls it and no mistake!"

"Get yourselves into the compartment," said the old photographer, ushering his grandchildren and Millie towards the train. "I'd better pop along to the booking office and obtain a ticket for this young woman, or she won't be able to accompany us."

Minutes later, all four of them were seated in their second-class compartment, waiting for the train to start.

Gerald, sitting in a corner-seat by the platform, glanced across towards the milk-churns and wondered whether Spelbush had started out on his long journey.

Grandfather Garstanton, at the other end of the compartment, was deep in his copy of the *Photographic Camera* while Millie, sitting opposite him, her bundle on the seat beside her, was gazing contentedly out of the window at the platform on the opposite side of the station.

Philippa, who occupied the window-seat opposite her brother, suddenly sat upright, wide-eyed and open-mouthed. She nudged one of Gerald's feet and nodded towards Millie's bundle. Gerald, following his sister's gaze, was equally amazed to see two small heads appear out of the top of the sheet-wrapped bundle and look around the carriage.

Fistram and Brelca, seeing the bundle as a means of escape from the boarding-house, had hidden themselves inside its folds while it was in the hall.

But the children's delight turned quickly to concern as they remembered something.

"Spelbush!" muttered Gerald.

Philippa nodded, urgently.

"All aboard!" called the guard, walking along the platform, slamming carriage-doors.

To his grandfather's astonishment, Gerald suddenly leaped to his feet, opened the door and jumped out.

"Hey! Gerald!" called Mr Garstanton as his grandson disappeared across the platform. Then, turning to his grand-daughter, the old man added: "What *does* your brother think he's up to?"

Philippa shook her head and shrugged, pretending that she had no idea.

Gerald, meanwhile, had begun to search for Spelbush in

the area where he had put him down only minutes before.

"Get back inside that train, boy!" shouted the guard, hurrying back along the platform in Gerald's direction. "Close that door!"

"Come back at once, Gerald! D'y'hear!" called his grandfather who was standing at the open door of the compartment.

But Gerald, peering around behind the milk-churns, paid no attention either to his grandfather or the guard.

"There you are!" he cried, happily, spotting Spelbush at last at the foot of a red penny-chocolate-bar machine. Then, swooping up the little man in his hands, he added: "It's all right. We've got your friends." Slipping Spelbush into his pocket, Gerald raced back across the platform.

"Count yourself lucky, young man, you didn't get left behind—*and* reported to the authorities," said the angry guard, slamming the door as Gerald jumped into the compartment.

He grinned, apologetically, as he sat down in his seat. "Sorry, Grandfather," he said, "I thought I'd left my cap behind—but it was in my pocket all the time!"

Grandfather Garstanton let out a sigh, shook his head— there were times when he just *didn't* understand children— and retired again behind the pages of his *Photographic Camera*.

"Boys will be boys," said Millie with a smile and turned her attention back outside the window.

The guard waved his flag, blew a shrill blast on his silver whistle, and jumped up into the guard's van as the train jerked, twice, and then moved slowly forward.

Fistram and Brelca, chancing another peep out of Millie's bundle, were overjoyed to see Spelbush grinning at them from Gerald's pocket.

Gerald and Philippa exchanged happy smiles.

The train picked up speed as it left the seaside town behind and rattled out into the countryside beyond, past farms and villages, broad fields and leafy woods.

7

The train pulled into the bustling city station with a grinding of brakes and a shrill scream from its whistle.

"Porter! I say, porter!" called Mr Garstanton, leaning out of the compartment window and bellowing across the platform.

"Yes, sir! Coming, sir!" replied the uniformed man, touching his cap with his forefinger before opening the door of the railway-carriage.

"Be careful with that photographic equipment," said Mr Garstanton, pointing up at the bags and boxes on the luggage-rack before stepping out on to the platform.

"Don't you worry, sir! Leave it all to me, sir," replied the porter, proffering a hand to Philippa who was following her grandfather.

Gerald, about to step down after his sister, first carefully handed her a carpet-bag which she accepted with equal care.

"Shall I take that, miss?" asked the obliging porter.

"No, thank you very much," said Philippa, clutching the carpet-bag all the more tightly.

Millie, holding her sheet-wrapped bundle in both hands, was the last of the Garstanton group to get down on to the platform. The porter stepped up into the empty compartment and started lifting down the luggage from the racks.

As Millie followed Mr Garstanton across the station towards the hansom-cab rank, Philippa opened the carpet-bag and she and Gerald peered inside.

The three little people, who had clambered into the carpet-bag during the railway journey, were sitting cross-legged on some folded clothing at the bottom of the bag blinking at the light and gazing up, enquiringly, at the children.

"Just what have you got in there?"

It was Mr Garstanton who had spoken. He had retraced his steps in order to discover why his grandchildren weren't following him.

"Nothing, Grandfather," gulped Philippa, hastily closing the carpet-bag and shaking her head.

"Nothing? It must be *something*! You've been hugging that bag between the two of you since Peterborough, as carefully as if it contained a clutch of eggs. What is it?"

Philippa and Gerald looked towards each other for inspiration.

"Starfish—" said Philippa.

"Sea-shells—" said Gerald.

"Starfish? Sea-shells?" echoed their grandfather, gruffly. "What are you starting up? A marine biology collection? Give it here—let me have a look!"

Philippa drew back, nervously, holding the carpet-bag close to her body. Mr Garstanton took a step towards her, putting out his hand to take the bag.

Then, just at the moment when it seemed that the secret of the little people would be revealed, the porter stumbled out of the carriage and almost fell on to the platform, his arms full of photographic equipment and his legs entangled in the camera's tripod.

"Look out for that camera!" exlaimed Mr Garstanton, turning round in some agitation. "It's an extremely valuable scientific instrument!"

"Safe as houses, sir!" said the porter as he succeeded in regaining his balance. "Will y'r honour be requiring a cab?"

Mr Garstanton nodded and, happily, the carpet-bag and its contents were forgotten for the moment.

Not long afterwards, the bag was stacked along with the rest of the luggage on top of a horse-drawn cab which rattled through the cobbled streets of the city with the three Garstantons and Millie, the maid, inside. As the cab-driver flicked his whip and the dappled mare picked up speed, the carpet-bag was jolted and tossed around on the roof of the cab until it seemed that it might tumble off into the road at any moment.

But the journey was soon over.

"Whoa there, Dolly! *Whoa* now!" called the cab-man, reining in his horse at the end of a row of tall town-houses.

The last house in the street, where the cab had drawn up, was situated next to a shop-front with a red-velvet-curtained window. Across the window in bold gold lettering was inscribed the legend:

RALPH GARSTANTON, ESQUIRE
CAMERA PHOTOGRAPHIST
By Appointment Only

"'Ere we are then, guvnor," cried the cab-driver, "'ome at last—all safe and sound!"

Gerald, Philippa, their grandfather and Millie, all stepped down on to the pavement and waited for the cabbie to pass down their belongings.

"One for you, sir," called the cabbie, handing down the first item of luggage.

Mr Garstanton took the trunk and placed it on the pavement. The next article to arrive was Millie's sheet-wrapped bundle of possessions which she put next to Mr Garstanton's trunk. Gerald was standing with open arms ready to receive the carpet-bag but, instead, the cabbie passed down the cumbersome wooden camera.

"'Ere you are, young master," said the cab-man.

"Careful now, Gerald," warned Mr Garstanton. "Keep a safe hold on it!"

Gerald took the camera in both hands and placed it, gently, on the pavement. The cabbie next took up the carpet-bag.

"And 'ere's a light one for you, missie," he called down to Philippa, swinging the carpet-bag in one hand and adding: "*Catch!*"

"*Don't!*" cried Philippa.

But her call came too late.

The cabbie had already let go of the carpet-bag which

sailed through the air towards Philippa who, in her anxiety, missed it completely. The bag struck the pavement with a horrendous hollow thud.

"Oh, no . . ." groaned Gerald, aghast.

"What's this, then?" chuckled Grandfather Garstanton, surprised at the extent of the children's concern for the contents of the carpet-bag. "Don't sea-shells and starfish bounce?"

Gerald did not hear. He knelt down and opened the carpet-bag, hardly daring to look inside, afraid of what he might see. But as Philippa joined him, Gerald gave her a reassuring glance and opened the carpet-bag a little wider.

Apart from clothing, there was nothing inside.

Then, as the children puzzled over what had happened, Gerald heard a tapping noise close at hand. Glancing down, he realized that the sound was coming from inside the camera that he had put carefully on the ground.

Lifting it up, he was surprised to see Fistram's face, distorted through the magnifying lens, peering out at him from inside the big wooden box. And, behind Fistram, two other tiny faces stared out.

"They must have taken it into their heads to move into safer lodgings while they were up on the cab-roof," he whispered to his sister.

Philippa, relieved, smiled and nodded.

While all of this had been going on, their grandfather had paid off the hansom cabbie and had got the rest of the luggage together, ready to take it into the house.

"Home again," said Grandfather Garstanton, looking

approvingly at the front door of the house which joined on to the photographic studio.

The children too were happy to be back.

"Mid pleasures and palaces though we may roam," recited Philippa, solemnly, "Be it ever so humble, there's no place like home."

"That front doorstep could do with a visit from the scrubbing-brush," said Millie, her thoughts on more domestic matters. "*And* them windows wouldn't come to no 'arm neither if they was to come face to face with a bucket of 'ot water and a window-leather."

Gerald, keeping a tight hold on the camera and its precious contents, grinned at Philippa. "East, West—home's best," he said.

The three Garstantons and their new maid moved to enter the house as Grandfather Garstanton felt in his trouser-pocket for the front-door key.

Some time later that same afternoon, the three little people stood and gazed around, surveying their new surroundings. They were standing in the living-room of Philippa's dolls' house which was situated on the top floor of the Garstanton home in the children's nursery. But even though the dolls' house and its furniture were more or less the right size for the little people, they seemed far from happy with their accommodation.

"It's not what I'd call *home*," said Brelca, running her fingers along the keys of a doll-size piano and getting no sound. The instrument's keyboard was only paint.

"It's not good enough," said Spelbush huffily.

"This door isn't real either," said Fistram, trying a door-handle and discovering that both the door *and* the handle were also no more than painted decorations.

The three little people turned towards the open front of the dolls' house and looked out at Gerald and Philippa who were both kneeling on the nursery carpet, watching them.

"It's just not good enough," repeated Spelbush, firmly. "It just won't do!"

"Those curtains will have to go," said Brelca with a shudder, pointing to the brightly coloured curtains which Philippa had stitched herself out of scraps from the sewing-basket.

"Nothing works in here at all," objected Fistram, tugging at the drawers of the sideboard which proved to be fake like everything else. "Everything's *pretend*!" he added.

"I think you're three very ungrateful little people!" snapped Philippa, who was extremely proud of the dolls' house and all its contents.

"It's not a question of gratitude, young lady," said Spelbush, loftily. "It's a question of what *is* acceptable on the one hand and, on the other hand, what is *not* acceptable. I am Spelbush Frelock, diplomatic emissary to his most imperial majesty, Emperor Golbasto Momaren Evlame Gurdilo Shefin Mully—"

"Ully Gue the seventeenth—we *know*!" interrupted Gerald and Philippa together.

For a moment, it seemed as if the little man would explode with anger, but he managed to contain himself, apart from going bright red in the face. "I must complain in the strongest terms that the accommodation, as provided, is ill-befitting my personage, my position and my dignity!" he announced, importantly.

He sat down on a wooden doll's chair with as much dignity as he was able to muster—only to find himself deposited on the floor as one of the chair-legs collapsed beneath him.

"Oh, *very* dignified, Spelbush," said Brelca with a grin, while Fistram sniggered.

Spelbush scrambled to his feet, redder in the face and angrier than ever.

"You *knew* that would happen!" he stormed at the children. "You put that chair there deliberately—you knew that it had a broken leg!"

"That was *your* fault!" said Philippa, turning on Gerald, crossly.

"No, it wasn't!"

"Yes, it was! You broke it off!"

The three little people listened and watched in polite silence as Gerald and Philippa ignored their visitors completely and engaged themselves in a brother-and-sisterly argument.

"I didn't break it off on purpose," snapped Gerald, picking up the chair and examining the broken leg. "It came off by accident when I was playing at the Battle of Balaclava with my toy soldiers—it was part of the barricades and it got struck by a lance from one of my Light Brigade."

"It's a chair!" stormed Philippa. "It's *not* a barricade! It's my doll's chair and it belongs to my dolls' house! And if you wanted to borrow it you should have asked permission."

"Like you asked me, I suppose," said Gerald, coldly, "when you cut a huge piece out of my butterfly-net to make a stupid veil for your silly doll's hat!"

"I didn't ask you first, Gerald, because I knew you would have refused me if I had," retorted Philippa. "And if you must know, I only did it to spoil your horrid net in the first place. It's cruel to stick pins in butterflies."

"I wasn't going to stick pins in them. I was going to keep them alive in a glass case."

"And that's wrong too! It's just as cruel to catch little things and keep them as pets—" Philippa broke off, remembering the three Lilliputians listening to the conversation which seemed to be verging on dangerous ground.

Brelca, Fistram and Spelbush had wandered out of the dolls' house and were gazing up at the children with raised eyebrows.

All five of them decided that it might be wise to change the subject.

"And another thing," said Brelca, looking up at the bedrooms of the dolls' house, "how are we supposed to get upstairs?"

"Easily," said Philippa. "I'll lift you up when it's time for you to go to bed."

In order to demonstrate her point, Philippa picked up Brelca and Fistram, one in either hand, and deposited them on the upper floor. When Spelbush's turn arrived he kicked and struggled in Philippa's grasp.

"Put me down, miss! Put me down, I say!" he shouted.

"If I am to be incapable of making my own way to my sleeping quarters, it would be better if I stay awake!"

Just at that moment, while Spelbush was still kicking and complaining in Philippa's hand, the nursery door opened and Millie bustled in clutching a bucket of firewood and a shovelful of glowing coals.

"'Ot coals!" she cried, cheerfully. "I should think you'll be needin' a fire in 'ere, else you'll both be chilled to the marrer-bone!"

And, without glancing towards the children, Millie swept across to the fireplace, tipped the burning coals into the empty grate and piled the firewood on top.

Philippa had time to pop Spelbush into the dolls' house with his companions without being noticed.

"You two ain't backwards in coming forwards," said Millie, still fussing at the fireplace.

"I don't know what you mean," said Gerald.

"Why—all *this*!" replied the housemaid, glancing admiringly around the spacious nursery with its cheerful wallpaper and comfortable furnishings. "I reckons as 'ow you've picked the nicest room in the 'ole 'ouse!" Her gaze wandered to the large dappled rocking-horse underneath the window, the toy-fort heavily defended by wooden soldiers by the open toy-cupboard and, lastly, the tall dolls' house on the carpet where the children were kneeling. "An' such *grand* toys too!" she continued, admiringly. "Just look at that there dollies' 'ouse!"

Philippa hastily closed the front of the house and slipped home the catch as Millie got to her feet, wiping coal-dust from her hands, and came towards them.

"Is it as h'elligant on the inside as it looks to be on the out?" asked Millie, peering at the wooden building.

"Not at all," said Gerald, shaking his head hurriedly. "It's empty at the moment."

"Vacant possession," added Philippa. "It's waiting for a new tenant."

"Garn! Don't you tease me!" scoffed the housemaid, bending down for a closer look through the windows. "Carpets an' curtains, I'll be bound, an' tiny furniture in ev'ry single room—"

Inside the dolls' house, the three little people reacted in panic. They scurried about on the upper floor and then, realizing they were trapped, they suddenly stiffened themselves into doll-like postures. All three of them remained quite still as one of Millie's eyes squinted in at the bedroom window.

"Oh my, ain't that a picture now!" she squealed. "An' bless me, if there ain't dear little dollies too to match! Don't they look *real*!"

The Lilliputians held their breath and stood as still as statues.

"'Ow does it open up then?" demanded Millie, taking her eye away from the window and feeling round the side of the wooden building for the catch that opened up the entire front. "Let's 'ave a proper look inside."

The two children exchanged a look of desperation and then, luckily, Gerald spotted a solution out of the corner of his eye.

Thick clouds of grey-black smoke were pouring out of the fireplace into the nursery.

"Millie!" cried Gerald. "Look at the fire!"

"Lawks-a-mercy!" cried the housemaid, jumping up and forgetting the dolls' house. She sped across the room and pulled and pushed at the "damper" which controlled the chimney-flue. "Enough smoke on the go for a boxful of kippers!" she said, coughing and spluttering. Happily, her efforts were rewarded and the smoke began to clear. "Hey, speaking of kippers—that reminds me of what else I came upstairs for!" she went on, waving a hand in front of her face to dispel the last of the smoke. "There's boiled cod and parsley sauce keeping warm in the kitchen. Shall you come downstairs, the pair of you—or am I to fetch you up a nursery-tea?"

Philippa and Gerald looked first at the dolls' house and then at each other. Simultaneously, they arrived at the decision that it would be wiser to keep Millie out of the nursery and away from the dolls' house—at least for the time being.

"We'll come downstairs with you," said Gerald.

"We can help you carry things," said Philippa, picking up the coal-shovel.

Gerald, taking the hint from his sister, took hold of the coal-bucket and then gently steered the housemaid towards the door.

"My, my, my! We *are* being helpful! What's brought this on all of a sudden?" asked Millie, allowing herself to be propelled on to the landing.

The door closed behind them.

Inside the dolls' house, the three tiny people had been watching events anxiously through an upper storey window. Now that the nursery was empty again, Fistram ran across to the bedroom window of the dolls' house and tried to push it open. But the task proved impossible.

"Nothing in this place is real!" said Fistram. "Everything in here is painted on!"

"Supposing it *did* work," said Spelbush looking down out of the window. "How would you propose that we manage the drop—*jump*?"

"We could easily knot some sheets together," replied Fistram.

"It wouldn't be *that* easy," said Brelca as she examined one of the beds. "The sheets are painted on as well! Even *this* is just pretend," she continued, sitting down at the dolls' dressing-table and picking up the tiny hairbrush. "It's made of *cardboard*. And the dressing-table mirror's not real either—it's only silver paper. I haven't seen myself in a mirror for *days*! I must look *awful*!"

Fistram, in his frustration, threw himself time and time again at the front wall of the house. But the catch that secured the front to the side wall held fast.

"This whole adventure's been a total disaster!" wailed Brelca.

"That's not true—" replied Spelbush.

"But it *has*!" insisted Brelca, cutting him short. "We set out to conquer a continent—and just look at us! We thought we'd be going home to heroes' welcomes. I'd expected to get a decoration. Brelca Reldresal—O.L.E.! The Order of the Lilliputian Empire! It's the dearest sweetest silver medal with an apple-green ribbon. I pictured myself waltzing at the Imperial Palace in my long red ball-dress with the entire court casting envious glances at my new apple-green ribbon . . ." She broke off, sniffed, blinked away a tear, and then continued: "Instead of which we're stuck here—seven seas away from home—and at the mercy of a pair of stupid children who provide silver-paper mirrors and cardboard painted hairbrushes."

In her anger, Brelca picked up the offending hairbrush and threw it across the room where it struck a painted window-sill and fell to the floor.

"It was a decision that we were all three agreed upon," said Spelbush, attempting to soothe Brelca. "We're following a carefully worked-out plan. We agreed that our best course of action—for the time being, at least—lies in staying with the children."

"We didn't know when we agreed to it that they'd be so . . . so childish!" said Brelca.

Brelca and Spelbush broke off their argument to turn and look at Fistram who had given up throwing himself at the front wall of the dolls' house and was now banging his head against it, childishly. Then, becoming aware of the disapproving glances of his two companions, he stopped, twiddled his thumbs, and gave them a foolish grin.

"We *had* to move on somewhere," Spelbush continued, looking at each of the others in turn. "We couldn't have stayed where we were. That Harwell Mincing man knew far too much by half! And this place is luxury indeed compared with what might have befallen us had we ended up in that villain's clutches. At least we're better off than that. Well? Admit it? Aren't we?"

Brelca and Fistram looked at each other, shuffled their feet and then finally nodded their heads.

"I suppose we are," said Brelca.

"I suppose we are . . ." echoed Fistram.

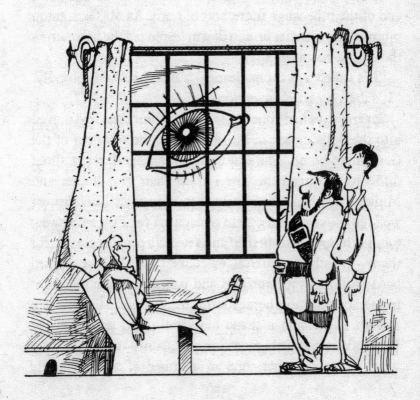

8

Millie watched, dutifully but rather doubtfully, as Mr Garstanton pumped hard at a curious big red metal cylinder which had a strange long tube attached to it. On the other end of the tube was a funny sort of horn. As Mr Garstanton pumped the cylinder up and down, he moved the horn across the dining-room carpet.

"It's called a vacuum cleaner, Millie," he said, proudly. "It's the very latest invention."

Several days had gone by since the Lilliputians had moved into the dolls' house in the nursery on the top floor of the Garstanton home. The children had managed, not without difficulty, to keep the secret from their grandfather and Millie. They had also contrived to keep their little visitors well fed—even to the extent of catering for Fistram's sweet tooth. Philippa had stitched and sewed to provide clothes for them—mostly for Brelca, of course! Gerald had worked hard with his woodwork-set and paints to make the dolls' house a comfortable home for the little people to live in, even though it *was* just a shade too small. But, all in all, the Lilliputians had little cause for complaint—although there were occasions when one or another of them (mostly

Fistram) suffered from homesickness.

Millie too had settled in quite happily. Working for Mr Garstanton, she quickly discovered, was much nicer than being in employment with Miss Mincing. Even so, there were moments when the photographer's love for new inventions rather puzzled the housemaid.

This was one of them.

"There!" exclaimed Mr Garstanton at last, breathless but triumphant. "What do you say to that, Millie?"

"Well, sir—it *looked* very energetic. But what was it all in aid of?"

"I've already told you! It's called a vacuum cleaner."

"I knows what you says it's *called*, sir. But what I don't know yet is what it's *for*?"

"I would have thought that was obvious," replied Mr Garstanton, rather gruffly. "It sucks up dirt. It cleans the carpets."

"Does it indeed, sir?" Millie sounded less than impressed.

"I understand that her majesty Queen Victoria has had several of them installed at Buckingham Palace—and Balmoral," said Mr Garstanton, proudly.

"That she may 'ave done, God bless 'er, but she's got the staff at them there palaces to work the blessed things," argued Millie. "There's only me 'ere to do it on my own. I ain't got time to go 'umping that around the 'ouse, sir— beggin' y'r pardin."

"It's intended to cut *down* the housework, Millie," explained Mr Garstanton.

Judging by the disappointed look on her employer's face,

Millie realized he was sad that she had been less than enthusiastic over his latest acquisition. "Well, if it will please you, sir, I'll give it a try at least, eh? But if you was to ask my opinion, I'd say it won't never replace a good stiff broom—" Millie broke off as she heard a sound from outside in the street. "Is that another of them army bands?" she said.

"I do believe it is," replied Mr Garstanton, putting down the big red cylinder and listening attentively. He walked across the dining-room and flung open the window. The sound of the military band could now be heard quite plainly, even though it was some way off.

Mr Garstanton and Millie leaned out of the window and looked along the street but there was no sign of any soldiers.

"It's no good, Millie. We shan't see them. They must be marching along Gladstone Street."

"That's the third lot that's gone off to South Africa this week," said Millie, rather sadly. "I see'd one regiment of lads marching into the railway station yesterday. Some of 'em. wornt no more than boys. Poor lads! Poor lads!"

Mr Garstanton and Millie withdrew their heads and closed the window behind them. They were neither of them aware that on the floor above, the nursery window was also open and that the children and the Lilliputians were also peering out along the street towards the sound of the military band.

Gerald and Philippa were leaning out of the window while Spelbush, Brelca and Fistram were outside in the nursery's window-box which they often used as a garden. Brelca and Fistram were standing on tiptoe, waving frantically towards the sound of the music, but Spelbush considered himself too grand for that kind of behaviour.

"I can't imagine for the life of me, why you two have to make such a fuss," he sniffed, loftily. "They're *streets* away from here, you know. They can't possibly see you waving."

"They're brave men, Spelbush," observed Brelca. "They're going off to fight a war—they deserve a wave whether they can see us or not."

"So?" said Spelbush, drawing an imaginary sword. "I don't consider that I myself am lacking in courage if put to the test—" As he spoke, he made a few tentative lunges with his imaginary blade at an equally imaginary enemy. Then, as his imaginary foe parried his blows, Spelbush took several steps backwards, neatly.

"AaaAAAGGGHHH!" he cried in alarm as his backward movement took one of his feet over the edge of the window-box. For one hair-raising split-second Spelbush teetered clumsily off-balance high above the street.

It was Gerald who reached out a hand, in the nick of time, and saved the Lilliputian from disaster.

"Careful!" said Gerald.

"I wasn't in any danger, you know," said Spelbush, after he had regained his breath. "I happen to have a perfect sense of balance." But, all the same, he moved several steps away from the rim of the window-box.

"I think it's time we went back indoors," said Philippa, wisely.

Once inside the nursery, the children carried the little people across to the table where all five of them had been playing at Snakes and Ladders before the stirring sounds of the military band had disturbed their game.

Spelbush picked up both dice in his arms and, using all his strength, bowled them across the table-top.

"Double-six!" he cried, gleefully.

But Gerald's thoughts were still on the soldiers going off to war. "I wish I was old enough to join the army," he said.

"You ought to be glad you're not," advised Philippa. "Many a one of those brave lads, so Millie says, will die a hero's death on foreign shores."

"Better to die a hero than live a coward," said Gerald.

"Who says that?" asked Philippa.

"It's in my book of *A Hundred-and-One Brave Deeds*—" Gerald broke off as he caught sight of Fistram who had huge tears rolling down both his cheeks. "Cheer up, Fistram!" Gerald continued, in the belief that the little man's thoughts, like his own, were with the soldiers marching off to war. "They're the British Infantry. The Soldiers of the Queen. They're not dead yet! They'll give the Boers what for!"

"I'm not crying for them," sobbed Fistram. "I'm crying for *me*. *I* don't want to die on foreign shores either."

Gerald and Philippa exchanged a troubled glance.

The thought of all the British soldiers going off to fight on foreign shores had reminded Fistram of his own predicament—far, far away from his native soil and no immediate hope of returning home.

"Are you *very* homesick, Fistram?" asked Philippa.

The little man nodded, dolefully. "Sometimes, for hours on end, I think of nothing else."

"How about you, Brelca?" asked Gerald. "Do you want to go home too?"

Brelca considered the prospect. "It would be nice to see a few old friends," she said. "And to go into a shop where everything was my size," she added, wistfully.

"What's the good of dreaming dreams," said Spelbush. "We *can't* go back—and that's that!"

"We could, if we had a seaworthy craft to sail in," said Fistram. "Like the *Antelope*."

"But we haven't," insisted Spelbush. "And even if we had a vessel, we're miles and miles away from the sea."

An awkward silence fell around the nursery table.

Philippa, in an attempt at lightening the gloom, picked up Spelbush's Snakes and Ladders counter and moved it forward twelve spaces. "Look!" she said. "You've landed on a ladder, Spelbush! You're going up three whole rows!"

But even that news didn't seem to cheer the Lilliputian.

"We're not miles away from the river, you know," said Gerald, who had been thinking hard. "And the river runs into the sea."

Brelca and Fistram looked hopeful.

"We wouldn't try to stop you going—if your hearts are really set on it," said Philippa.

"We'd still need to find a ship," said Fistram.

"That shouldn't be impossible," said Gerald.

"It's not just a question of not stopping us," said Brelca. "Could we count on you to help us?"

"Of course you could!" said the children in unison, without hesitation.

Moments later, watched by the three little people, the children were on their knees ransacking the lower shelves of the toy-cupboard. Philippa unearthed a tin-plate rowing-boat complete with a clockwork oarsman who, when his spring was wound up, could propel his little craft across water.

"There's this!" she said.

"That's no good, Phil!" said Gerald.

But the little people were intrigued by the clockwork toy.

"What does it do?" asked Fistram.

Philippa wound up the clockwork mechanism and then released her hold on the key. The oarsman, who was about the same size as a Lilliputian, rowed furiously for about thirty seconds before slowly coming to a stop. Brelca and Fistram were both delighted with the toy, but Spelbush was unimpressed.

"My dear good child, that isn't any use at all!" he said to Philippa, impatiently. "We're looking for a craft that could convey us across oceans—not a child's tin-plate toy!"

"He's right—for once," said Gerald.

"I'm always right," said Spelbush in his most infuriating voice.

"Nobody's *always* right," snapped Philippa.

"I'm older than you, and therefore wiser," said Spelbush airily and then, turning to his companions, he continued: "How can we possibly go back? We came to these shores as explorers—colonizers—*conquerors*! How can we go back now when all we have to tell our countrymen is that we made the acquaintance of a pair of little children!"

"*Little* children! I like that!" said Gerald.

"Oh, don't be such a spoilsport, Spelbush!" said Philippa, angrily. After all, she had only been trying to cheer up the Lilliputians with the clockwork toy and take Fistram's mind off his homesickness. "Surely we can *play* at boats," she went on. "I thought we might put the rowing-boat in the bath."

"What a good idea!" said Fistram, his spirits rising at the thought.

"There's no harm in that, is there, Spelbush?" said Brelca, catching Fistram's change of mood.

"Why don't we, Gerald?" said Philippa.

"Why not?" said Gerald. "You go along to the bathroom, Phil, and make a start. I'll join you when I've found what I'm looking for."

Philippa scooped up Brelca, Fistram and the clockwork rowing-boat. "Come along," she said, making for the door.

But Spelbush folded his arms and made no move to join them. Instead, he gazed at Gerald whose head was deep inside the toy-cupboard.

As Philippa came out of the nursery, her arms bulging with the little people and the tin-plate toy, she almost walked into Millie who was busy at the top of the stairs.

Luckily, the housemaid was too busy at her task to notice what Philippa was carrying. Millie's head was bent over the new vacuum cleaner which she was pumping vigorously with both hands, cleaning the stair-carpet.

"Where are you off to, Miss Philippa?" said Millie, without glancing up.

"Only to the bathroom, Millie," replied Philippa as she sidled past, hugging the little people close to her body and keeping her back turned to the housemaid.

"What for?"

"Just to sail a boat." As she spoke, Philippa hopped down two stairs at once in an effort to get away from Millie as quickly as was possible.

And now, tired from her exertions with the vacuum cleaner, the housemaid *did* glance up as she paused for breath. "Don't you dare make any mess in that there bathroom, Miss Philippa," she cautioned at Philippa's fast-retreating back. "I've on'y just finished scrubbing it out in there, not an hour since." But Philippa was out of sight and earshot before the maid had finished her warning. Millie frowned as she went back to pumping the vacuum cleaner. "I still says as 'ow a good stiff broom would do this job better!" she grumbled to herself.

Once in the bathroom, Philippa set Brelca and Fistram down on the edge of the bath and turned on the cold tap.

The Garstanton bathroom was a grand affair, recently installed, all gleaming marble and polished copper. There was a copper shower too over the bath, another recent invention which was Grandfather Garstanton's pride and joy.

"Me first! Me first!" cried Fistram, jumping up and down on the rim of the bath excitedly as Brelca wound up the rowing-boat's clockwork motor.

"Wait a minute!" scolded Philippa as she turned off the tap.

Then, picking up the Lilliputian, she sat him on the stern of the rowing-boat where he was able to link his arms around the oarsman's waist. Next, Philippa floated the boat gently at one end of the bath and released the clockwork mechanism.

The tin-plate oarsman's arms reached out, jerkily, and dipped the oars in the bathwater.

"Hold on tight, Fistram!" cried Brelca, who was still sitting on the edge of the bath.

The clockwork man gained speed as his arms shot back and forth and the little boat sped the length of the bath in no time at all. The craft struck the far end of the bath, hard, dislodging Fistram and depositing him in the water. A moment later, he surfaced, dripping wet but with a wide grin across his face.

"Let's try it again," he said, having plainly enjoyed the experience.

"Don't be so impatient, Fistram," scolded Philippa. "It's Brelca's turn next."

"That's quite all right," said Brelca, who had no great wish for a drenching. "I'll wait—Fistram can go again if he pleases."

As Fistram nodded happily, Philippa lifted the rowing-boat out of the bath and began to rewind the clockwork motor.

Meanwhile, in the nursery on the floor above, Gerald had laid his hands at last on what he had been looking for.

"Found it!" he murmured to himself as he reached into the very back of the toy-cupboard and drew out the model yacht he had been given on his birthday two years before.

The yacht was a sleek-lined scale model, carved by a craftsman out of finest beechwood and complete with working sails and ropes. It had been Gerald's favourite toy for over a year. He had carried it, lovingly, into the park every weekend and sailed it, proudly, on the boating-lake. But then the yacht had finally fallen out of favour when it had been replaced by a large dragon-kite that Gerald had received at Christmas. For over a year now, the yacht had remained hidden at the back of the toy-cupboard, buried underneath a pile of toys.

It was exactly what was needed now, he thought. It was just the right size to take a crew of Lilliputians. Gerald scrambled to his feet and ran towards the nursery door, cradling the yacht in his arms. In his excitement he failed to notice Spelbush who had been standing watching him all this time.

"Hey!" called the Lilliputian. "Just a minute! What about me!"

But Gerald was already through the door.

Millie had now arrived at the top of the stair-carpet with the hand-pump vacuum cleaner. "I've already told your sister, Master Gerald—if you messes up that nice clean bathroom floor betwixt the two of you, I'll skin you both alive, so I will!"

But Gerald, taking the stairs two at a time, paid little heed to the housemaid's warning.

Millie, shaking her head and "tut-tutting" to herself, pumped even harder at the vacuum cleaner in her anger, without even looking at what she was doing.

As Gerald walked into the bathroom, Fistram was sitting on the side of the bath, using a face-cloth as a giant-size bath-towel. The little fellow's eyes lit up with joy when he saw the yacht the boy was carrying.

"That's *much* more like it!" said Fistram, as Gerald lowered the yacht into the bath where it floated, motionless, on the still water. "That'll take all three of us."

"Speaking of the three of us," said Brelca, with a frown, "where's Spelbush?"

Gerald and his sister exchanged a puzzled glance.

"I thought he was down here with you," said Gerald.

"I thought he was upstairs with you," said Philippa.

"Oh dear!" said Brelca.

A moment later, Gerald and Philippa were making their way, slowly, back up the staircase that led to the nursery. Gerald was carrying the towel-wrapped Fistram while Philippa held Brelca in both hands. All four of them examined each stair carefully.

"Spelbush?" They called the name out softly but urgently.

But there was no sign of the third member of the *Antelope*'s crew on the staircase and the children moved the search up into the nursery.

"And what might you pair be up to now?" asked Millie, who was vacuuming the nursery rugs.

"Nothing, Millie!" exclaimed the children together, surprised at seeing the housemaid. Quickly, they hid the little people behind their backs.

"Oh yes, you is!" replied the housemaid, sharply. "'Cos if

you *ain't* up to anything, why are you both looking so guilty, I'd like to know? And what have you both got 'idden be'ind your backs?"

The children hung their heads, said nothing, and looked guiltier than ever.

Luckily, Millie was too busy to pursue her questioning. "Never mind! Never mind!" she said briskly. "I ain't got time to listen. I've got to figure out 'ow to *empty* this contrivance now I've filled it!" Millie tucked the heavy vacuum cleaner canister under one arm, balancing it on her hip, as she added: "Talk about *making* work! I dunno!" She crossed to the nursery door where she paused for a final word. "An' this room's clean—so see as 'ow it stays clean— I'll bet you ain't 'arf made a mess in that there bathroom!" With which, she flounced from the room.

As soon as the door closed behind the housemaid, the children put the two little people down on the nursery floor and all four of them began the search.

"Spelbush!" called Gerald.

"Where are you?" cried Philippa.

Brelca searched the dolls' house and the toy-cupboard while Fistram looked underneath all the furniture. But there was no sign of Spelbush.

"He's gone," said Gerald, dolefully. "It's as if he'd disappeared off the face of the earth."

"It's as if he'd vanished into thin air," said Philippa.

"It's as if the ground had opened up and swallowed him," said Fistram.

Brelca's worried face appeared round the bottom of the

toy-cupboard door. An awful thought had just entered her mind. "You don't think he could have been swallowed up by something else, do you?"

Gerald's eyes widened and Philippa gulped as they both realized what Brelca was suggesting.

"Millie's vacuum cleaner!" they said together.

Leaving Brelca and Fistram to fend for themselves, the children raced through the nursery door and down the stairs.

Millie was already outside in the basement area where she had taken off the lid of the dustbin and, in a positive cloud of dust, was emptying the contents of the vacuum cleaner.

Gerald and Philippa ran down the last flight of stairs, hared across the hall and through the door that led into the kitchen.

Millie had replaced the dustbin-lid and walked back into the kitchen where she was almost bowled over by the children as they rushed past her.

"Lawks-a-mercy!" cried the housemaid. "Can't I go anywheres this morning without 'aving you pair under my feet!"

But Philippa and Gerald were already outside. Gerald lifted off the dustbin-lid, slowly, as if fearing the worst. But there was no need for him to worry. Spelbush, coughing and spluttering but otherwise safe and sound, was sitting on top of the rubbish with the dust-cloud settling around him.

"Are you all right, Spelbush?" asked Gerald.

"You haven't hurt yourself?" added Philippa.

"All right?" snapped the Lilliputian. "Of course I'm not all right! Do I *look* as if I'm all right?"

"It's his pride that's hurt, as usual," Philippa whispered to Gerald.

"I have never been so humiliated in my entire life," Spelbush continued. "I simply refuse to stay in this alien land an instant longer than is necessary! The sooner I and my comrades acquire a seaworthy craft and make all sail for home, the better I will like it!"

"We think we might have found you one already," said Gerald.

Not long after, once the dust had been brushed off Spelbush and the two other little people had been collected from the nursery, the children and the Lilliputians were back in the bathroom. Spelbush, Fistram and Brelca were standing on the deck of Gerald's yacht which lay becalmed, where the children had left it, on the calm clear water in the bath. Gerald and Philippa, kneeling by the side of the bath, were watching the little people anxiously, waiting to hear what Spelbush would have to say about the yacht.

The leader of the company of three frowned as he strode the length of the deck in half-a-dozen paces. "It isn't going to work, you know," he said, with a shake of his head.

"Why not?" said Gerald.

"It isn't big enough, for one thing."

"It's the biggest ship *we've* got," said Philippa, with a sigh.

"It isn't strong enough either," added Spelbush. "Supposing there was a storm at sea?"

"We can soon find out about that," said Gerald. "Hold on tight and I'll make one for you."

Gerald put a hand into the bath and swirled the water round and round. The yacht, following the current, picked up speed and careered around the bath, bumping against the side and rocking dangerously. But the little people were experienced sailors and, this time, even Fistram managed to keep his balance. To add to the storm in the bath-tub, Philippa turned the handle which controlled the flow of water through the gleaming copper shower over the bath.

Cold water poured down from a hundred eyelets in the shower-head, causing rain to lash the deck of the yacht. The little people clung on grimly as their craft pitched and tossed on the turbulent bathwater but, no matter how much of a storm was whipped up by the children, the model yacht rode it bravely without overturning.

At last, Gerald put out a hand and steadied the vessel.

"Well?" he said. "What do you think about her now?"

But, once again, Spelbush shook his head, slowly and firmly.

Some time later, after the three little people had dried themselves from their shower-bath rain-storm and were sitting, with the children, perched along the padded seat of the nursery fireguard, gazing solemnly into the leaping flames, Spelbush spoke at length about his doubts and fears concerning their proposed voyage.

"You see, my dear young friend," he concluded to Gerald, "there's an entire world of difference between riding out a storm in a bath-tub and facing up to the real-life dangers of the rolling deep."

"I don't see why?" said Gerald, reluctant to admit that his

model yacht was not capable of a seagoing trip. "She's an excellent craft—all I have to do is set her sails and she steers herself across the boating-lake." He looked to his sister for confirmation. "Isn't that true, Phil?"

"Every time!" said Philippa, nodding her head in agreement fervently.

Spelbush smiled. "At the risk of repeating myself," he said, importantly, "my companions and myself are contemplating crossing half a dozen oceans, young man—not a boating-lake!—we could *never* set out on such a voyage aboard a child's toy-boat!"

"It's *not* a toy!" said Gerald, hotly. "It's a craftsman-built model with each part made exactly to scale!"

"It's still a toy," said Spelbush.

"Of course it's a toy!" agreed Brelca. "It isn't *real*. It isn't for *grown-ups*. It's a *toy*. We're tired of having to make do with toys—it's the same as having to live in that ridiculous dolls' house!"

"And what, pray, is wrong with living in my dolls' house?" demanded Philippa, coldly. "It's just as I've always said—you're three *very* ungrateful little people! I wish I'd never lent you my dolls' house now!"

"There's nothing *wrong* with the dolls' house, little girl," said Spelbush, trying to calm the situation. "It's an extremely *nice* house."

"For dolls," put in Fistram.

"Exactly!" added Spelbush.

"But it's hopeless for real *live* people," said Brelca. "Nothing in it is *real*. Everything is *painted* on. The doors.

The drawers. The piano-keys. Even the looking-glass isn't a real looking-glass. It's only silver paper. I can't see to brush my hair. And even if the looking-glass *was* a looking-glass, I still wouldn't be able to brush my hair—the hairbrush is only a piece of cut-out painted cardboard!"

"And it's the same with the yacht," said Spelbush. "There are no real cabins. The cabin-door is painted on. You can't go inside it because there's nowhere inside to go."

"Where could we store our stores?" asked Fistram. "And if we can't store stores—what are we supposed to eat?"

"Or where are we supposed to keep our clothes?" said Brelca. "Or wash our hair? How could we keep up our appearances?"

"We really *couldn't* sail the seas in it, you know," said Spelbush, almost apologetically. "It just isn't good enough."

Gerald and Philippa turned and looked across at the model yacht and then back at the little people's earnest upturned faces. The children were forced to agree with the Lilliputians. The model yacht was just not good enough.

"If we are to be able to sail away," said Spelbush, "we must have a practicable working full-sized ship."

"*Our* size, of course," said Fistram.

"Full-sized *our* size—not yours," Brelca added, in case her companions' explanations had not been clear enough.

"A real ship, not a toy," said Spelbush. "But one that we can handle."

"I don't know where we could possibly find one of those," said Gerald, despondently.

"There aren't any," said Philippa.

"That's that, then," said Spelbush, equally gloomy. "We'd better forget the whole idea."

All five of them sighed, shrugged, and went back to staring into the nursery fire. They tried to forget their disappointment by playing one of their favourite games: looking for pictures in the glowing red coals.

"I can see a face!" said Brelca.

"Where?" asked Fistram.

"There!" said Brelca, pointing into the heart of the fire. She shuddered. "Oooh, it's horrible—the face of an evil man."

"I can't see anything," said Philippa.

"I can," said Gerald. "A thin-faced man with dark staring eyes. It reminds me of someone."

"Me too," said Brelca. "I wonder who?"

It would not be long before they found out. And, when they did, the Lilliputians would have more to think about than going home.

9

The gleaming steel-toothed jaws of the miniature man-trap snapped on to the pencil, sharply, breaking it in half. Harwell Mincing swung the tiny man-trap by its long, silver chain and chuckled softly to himself.

"What, in the name of heaven, is that contraption intended for?" asked Sarah Mincing, shuddering slightly.

The two Mincings were in the kitchen at 14 Khartoum Gardens. Harwell was sitting at the kitchen table with Sarah looking over his shoulder.

"It's a trap, of course," replied Harwell, testing the strength of the sharp, shining jaws with his thumbs. "I've had a number of them constructed by a friend of mine."

"He's no friend of mercy then, if he manufactures articles such as that for his living!" retorted Sarah. "And what poor dumb creatures do you propose to snare with them?"

"No poor dumb creatures, sister—but cunning, crafty, sly-booted things as sharp-witted almost as we are ourselves." He paused, and then added quietly: "Little people."

"Not that again!" snapped Sarah. "I thought that you'd put that harebrained nonsense behind you, days ago, after the Garstantons left."

"Is it harebrained nonsense to desire to pursue a fortune?" snarled Harwell, getting to his feet and warming his behind at the kitchen fire.

"Desire it all you will, brother. Pursue it if you must. Grasp it if you can. But I very much doubt you'll have the opportunity to spend it."

"Why not?"

"Why not, says he!" scoffed Sarah Mincing. "Because they'll lock you away, brother, as sure as eggs are eggs! There are poor unfortunates in the madhouse at this very minute who are more in possession of their senses than yourself! Little people, indeed! Merciful heaven, whatever next?"

"They exist, Sarah!" thundered Harwell. "Believe me, they exist! First there was their shipwreck off these shores— I have the ship's bell with their vessel's name upon it—then the hamper and the very dagger they used to cut the strap— how else do you explain a dagger of that size? I tell you, they sailed here all the way from Lilliput, wherever that may be, and they were in this house! And now those Garstanton brats have got them, I would stake my life upon it. Oh, but I shall track them down, Sarah. I shall trap them. And then I shall show them to the public and I shall make my fortune."

"God take pity on you, Harwell Mincing," said Sarah, solemnly. "How can a man show something to the public that exists only in his own fevered imagination? They are entirely of your own invention."

"Was my fattest woman in the world an invention? Were

my two-headed dog and my five-legged lamb inventions also?"

"Your fattest woman in the world was no more nor less than a common glutton, brother. And your five-legged lamb and two-headed dog were frauds—tricks of the taxidermist's art—fashioned with needle and with cobbler's twine. And well you know it. Aye, and not only frauds, Harwell, but also an affront to the Almighty."

"But these little people *are* real, Sarah. I swear it to you. Come with me."

"Come with you?" echoed his sister, puzzled. "Come with you where?"

"Close down this house for the next few months. Help me track down these Lilliputians and ensnare them. Why not, Sarah? What do you have to lose?"

"Only my sanity, as you've lost yours," snorted Sarah.

"But supposing I'm right, sister? What then?" said Harwell, rubbing his right thumb, gloatingly, against his fingertips. "You'll not make a penny here—a guest-house that boasts not a single guest."

"Only because the season is over," replied Sarah, scowling. "It's the end of the summer."

"That may well be so," said Harwell, a greedy smile lurking at the corners of his mouth. "But if I can only get my hands on those little creatures—it could signal the start of a summer of plenty for both you and me. What do you say?"

Sarah Mincing searched her brother's face with her eyes . . .

What she saw there must have convinced her that Harwell

was not entirely out of his mind. Before twenty-four hours had passed, Harwell and Sarah, surrounded by their luggage and dressed, as always, sombrely and sinisterly in black, were standing on the platform of their local railway station. They were waiting for the train which would take them to the town where, they knew, they would be able to track down the Garstantons.

"I lay all this while, as the reader may believe, in great uneasiness: at length, struggling to get loose, I had the fortune to break the strings, and wrench out the pegs that fastened my left arm to the ground—"

"Excuse me," said Brelca, interrupting Gerald who was reading aloud to the three small visitors. "But does it *really* say that?"

"See for yourself," said Gerald, holding up in front of Brelca's face the book that he had chosen from the nursery bookshelves.

"And is that supposed to have been written by Lemuel Gulliver as well?" asked Fistram, interrupting for the umpteenth time that afternoon.

"I've *told* you," said Gerald, turning the volume round and showing the little people the cover. "It's *Gulliver's Travels*. He wrote every word of it."

"Then that's something else that he made up," said Fistram.

"Made up?" echoed Philippa, in shocked tones.

Philippa and Gerald were sitting on the nursery rug in front of the fire while the three little people were perched, as usual, in a row on the nursery fireguard.

Fistram nodded, firmly. "He didn't break the strings at all. He *couldn't* have broken the strings. They were very *strong*. Our ancestors had him safely fastened to the ground. They *cut* him loose, out of the kindness of their hearts."

"It's written down in all our history books," agreed Spelbush. "It's an indisputable fact."

"History books don't lie," said Brelca, with a yawn. The children were finding it increasingly difficult to keep the little people out of sight *and* entertained. It had been Gerald's idea to read *Gulliver's Travels* to them, but it was not proving a success. They kept picking holes in Gulliver's story.

"Shall I go on?" asked Gerald, stiffly.

"No thanks," said Fistram. "I've heard enough."

"Me too," said Spelbush.

"Besides, it would take days and days to read all that," added Brelca, looking at the book which was taller than she was herself. "Just tell us how it ends."

"*I* know how it ends," said Philippa. "After he left Lilliput, Gulliver sailed to a land called Brobdingnag. It was full of giants."

"The same as himself," said Fistram.

"Oh, no," said Gerald, shaking his head. "Much bigger than himself—ten times bigger."

"Twenty times!" said Philippa.

"But *he* was a giant," said Brelca, puzzled.

"You can't have giants bigger than giants," said Fistram. "Giants *are* giants. If you ask me, it doesn't make sense."

"If you ask *me*, none of it makes sense," said Spelbush, loftily. "But then that was the principal reason we came to your country."

"Because of Gulliver?" asked Gerald.

"To retrace his voyage," said Spelbush, nodding. "We wanted to see if his charts were accurate. They'd been lying in our Maritime Museum for two hundred years, gathering dust. It was decided they should be tested."

"And now that we've proved this land exists," sighed Fistram, feeling homesick all over again, "we'd very much like to go back to Lilliput."

"After we've conquered it," said Spelbush.

"How about a game of Ludo?" suggested Philippa, hoping to stop the little people quarrelling and also to cheer up Fistram.

Gerald got out the Ludo board and the dice and counters and set them out on the nursery table. In next to no time, Gulliver and Lilliput and "going home" were all forgotten. Philippa, Gerald, Brelca, Spelbush and Fistram were all concentrating on Ludo.

Downstairs, in the photographic studio, the children's grandfather was hovering behind his camera and tripod and smiling, encouragingly, at two customers.

"If you'd be so good as to compose your features, Mr and Mrs Baxendale," he said. "Just look natural and make yourselves comfortable."

The middle-aged couple thus addressed, who were looking into a camera lens for the very first time in their lives, tried hard to smile. They weren't enjoying the experience one little bit. It was difficult to appear "composed and comfortable" when the backs of their heads, necks, elbows and various other limbs were held tight in rigid clamps invisible to the camera.

These clamps, of course, were used to keep the sitters still in an age when indoor photography required exposure-times of several seconds at the very least. Mr Garstanton, considering himself an artist, shunned the then current craze for flash-powder.

"Please adopt the expressions you would most desire the camera to capture for all time," continued the photographer, ducking his head beneath the black velvet cloth that was draped over the back of his camera. Once in the darkness beneath the velvet, Mr Garstanton peered into his viewfinder and gazed at the upside-down image of his customers.

Mrs Baxendale, a portly lady, was wearing an enormous flowered hat and sitting bolt upright in a chair. Mr Baxendale, a much smaller person altogether than his wife, had bushy side-whiskers and a flowing moustache. He was clutching his bowler hat to his chest with one hand, awkwardly, while balancing his chin on his other hand and resting his elbow, artistically, on a Grecian plinth.

Satisfied with his positioning of the couple Mr Garstanton ducked from underneath his velvet cloth and held his exposure bulb up in the air.

"Smile, please!" he said, pressing the bulb and then counting, slowly, up to ten. "That's it!" he said, releasing the bulb. "That's all there is to it! Not half as painful as you thought it was going to be, eh?"

Mr and Mrs Baxendale, gripped firmly by the clamps and already suffering agonies from pins-and-needles, were unable either to nod or shake their heads in answer to his question. "And I'll have your photographic-portrait ready for you by the end of the week," added the photographer, reaching out to tug at a bell-rope before going to release the grateful couple from the clamps.

Millie, mixing dough for bread down in the kitchen, glanced up at the row of bells connected with every room in the house. The one marked "Studio" was jangling, noisily. The housemaid wiped her hands on her apron and moved towards the door in answer to the summons.

Outside, on the opposite side of the street to the Garstanton home, a couple of black-garbed figures were standing in the shelter of a herbalist's shop doorway, keeping watch on the photographic studio.

"You're quite sure he's going out this afternoon?" asked Sarah Mincing of her brother. "You've made enquiries?"

"Made enquiries and double-checked on them," replied Harwell who was holding a leather Gladstone bag. "Every Wednesday afternoon, at two o'clock precisely, he closes his studio and attends the brass-band concert in the park."

"And what's the time now?"

Harwell Mincing took out his pocket-watch and flicked open the lid with his thumb-nail. "Five minutes to the hour," he said, and then, glancing across the street, he added: "Look!"

Sarah Mincing followed her brother's glance.

Mr Garstanton's face appeared above the curtain in the

window as he hung up a "Closed" sign.

"What did I tell you?" said Harwell, smiling grimly and slipping his watch back into his waistcoat pocket.

"And what about the brats?" asked Sarah. "Do they go with him?"

"No." Harwell shook his head. "They attend pianoforte lessons on Wednesday afternoons. The house is empty— save for some maid they've taken into their employ. Here come the clients now—"

Across the street, the door to the photographic studio had opened and Millie was giving the Baxendales a quick little curtsy as she ushered them into the street.

"Curse the idle slovenly wench—and curse our bad fortune!" said Sarah, sharply, her eyes widening in surprise. "It's Millie!"

"Millie?" asked Harwell, frowning. "Who's Millie?"

"Millie Lottersby, of course! You've met the slattern. She worked for me until last week."

"Then what's she doing here with the Garstantons?"

"As little as she can get away with, if I know that girl," snapped Sarah. "Aye, and no doubt laying on blacklead and floor-polish as if they grew on trees. Although her lack of concern for her employer's property is not the point at issue, brother. The hard fact is that you can't go near that house. The slut will recognize you for sure!"

"*Pah*—nonsense!" snarled Harwell. "She saw me for one brief instant only—and there's no milk spilt on that account." Harwell paused and patted his Gladstone bag. "I've taken that contingency into account. I've brought a disguise along with me. Leave everything to me, sister. But you should go now. At once—or you'll be recognized for certain."

Sarah hesitated and sucked at her cheek. "I'm still not sure that I want to be a party to this deed," she said.

"Say that again, sister, when we're sitting in the lap of luxury," urged her brother, coaxingly. "The richest show-people in the country. Nay, the world! Why—Phineas T. Barnum must be turning in his grave with envy! General Tom Thumb was a giant compared with the specimens we're about to cage. Go, now—quickly, Sarah. I'll see you back at our rooms."

And Sarah Mincing, impressed with her brother's words, left the shop doorway and walked purposefully off along the street, her stout black shoes clicking on the pavement. Harwell Mincing turned his attention to the house and studio opposite.

Millie, in the hall, was helping Mr Garstanton to put on his coat while the old gentleman called up the stairs.

"Come along, you prodigies!" he shouted. "You're late for piano-lesson! I promised your parents I'd see to it that you didn't neglect your musical studies!"

"Shan't be a moment, Grandfather!" Philippa yelled from the landing at the top of the house, her bulging music-case in her hand. "We're just looking for our practice-pieces!" She glanced back, anxiously, through the open nursery door to where Gerald, on his knees, was in urgent conversation with their three little visitors.

The Lilliputians were rebelling at the prospect of being

left all alone for the afternoon.

"We still don't understand why we can't come with you," grumbled Fistram, stamping his foot on the floor of the dolls' house and folding his arms.

"We need the exercise," said Spelbush.

"And the fresh air," added Brelca. "We've been cooped up in these four walls for days!"

"Eight walls to be precise," said Spelbush, correcting his companion and pointing first to the walls of the dolls' house and next to the walls of the nursery, saying: "There are these four walls and those four walls."

"You've had some exercise today already," argued Gerald. "We took you out this morning."

"Out?" snapped Brelca. "Out! Do you call that *out*? Ten measly minutes trudging round and round the nursery window-box. With those scruffy sparrows staring down at us from the opposite chimney-pots—looking at me all the time as if I was some sort of *worm*!" She shuddered and then added: "I hardly call *that* going out, young man!"

"We hardly call piano-lessons outings either," said Gerald. "And you know you wouldn't enjoy it anyway. You hate having to listen to Philippa thumping out her exercises—" He broke off and listened in some concern as his grandfather's voice floated up the stairs again.

"On parade, you piano-players! Last time of asking before I come up there and carry you down!"

"Coming, Grandpa!" Philippa called back from the nursery door before hissing at her brother: "Gerald! *Hurry!* We *must* go!"

Gerald looked down again at the three complaining Lilliputians. "We'll take you out into the garden the minute we get back," he said, pleadingly. "Won't we, Philippa?"

"Cross our hearts!" agreed his sister. "*And* we'll ask Millie if we can have a picnic-tea outside. There's Madeira cake and pink blancmange—I've seen them."

"Honestly, we won't be long," added Gerald. "An hour and a half at the very most."

The three little people looked at one another. The prospect of Madeira cake and pink blancmange was very enticing.

"Oh, very well," grumbled Spelbush, acting as usual as spokesman for the three.

Gerald closed the front of the dolls' house and slipped home the catch on the side wall, shutting in the little people until he and his sister returned home from their piano-lessons. The two of them raced down the stairs to where their grandfather waited, increasingly impatient, in the hall.

The house was silent save for the constant ticking of the longcase clock in the hall.

Millie was downstairs in the kitchen, attending to her baking.

The three little people sat inside the living-room of the dolls' house and gloomily contemplated their surroundings. An hour and a half seemed an awfully long time to have to wait. Fistram got to his feet and walked over to the mantelpiece where he picked up a tiny clock, looked at it, listened, and then shook it, hard.

"It's no good doing that," said Spelbush. "Those hands

are painted as well. That clock will say a quarter past five until the end of time."

Fistram shrugged and replaced the clock on the mantelpiece. "I suppose pink blancmange is worth waiting for," he observed.

"I don't doubt that it is," replied Spelbush, sharply, "for those of us who think of nothing else but their stomachs."

"I happen to be rather partial to pink blancmange," replied Fistram, taking offence at Spelbush's words.

"We all know how partial you are to pink blancmange, Fistram," said Brelca, hiding a smile. "The last time there was pink blancmange, you were so partial to it that you fell into the bowl!"

"That was an accident," said Fistram, frowning. "It could have happened to anyone."

"Be quiet, you two!" ordered Spelbush, who had gone to a corner of the room where he was examining the gap, not quite wide enough to slip his hand through, between the side wall and the hinged front of the house. He glanced around the room for some implement that might slide through the narrow aperture. His eyes fell on an object that looked as if it might suit the task he had in mind. "Pass me that poker, Brelca," he said.

Brelca handed Spelbush the tiny poker from the set of toy fire-irons in the dolls' house fireplace. He pushed one end of it through the gap and tried to unlatch the hook from the metal ring that kept them locked inside.

"Got it!" he cried at the third attempt, as the end of the poker connected with the tip of the hook and he moved it upwards and through the ring. "Now then! With me! All push together!" he said, putting his shoulder against the inside front wall of the dolls' house.

Brelca and Fistram put their backs with his and all three of them pushed hard. Slowly, the front of the dolls' house creaked open on its squeaky hinges. Then, as the Lilliputians walked forward with it, they found themselves out on the nursery floor.

It was the first time, since their arrival, that they had been free and unattended in the Garstanton home. They looked towards the nursery door which had been left open by the children in their haste. All three of the little people felt an urge to explore the building.

"But what if they come back?" said Fistram.

"We've got an hour and a half," said Brelca. "We could go over the entire house and still be back before they return."

"Ssshhh!" whispered Spelbush, holding up a warning finger at the sound of hurrying footsteps on the stairs.

"It's only the maid," said Brelca. "I heard her saying this morning that when she'd finished the baking she was going into the dining-room to clean the silver."

Sure enough, they heard the sound of a door being opened on the first floor and then, again, all was silent.

"Good!" exclaimed the delighted Spelbush. "We can go wherever we please—so long as we steer clear of the dining-room."

"There's an enormous bowl of fruit in the parlour," suggested Brelca.

"What are we waiting for?" said Fistram.

In no time at all, the three of them had crossed the upper landing and set off down the top flight of stairs. It was an exercise at which they were becoming, by now, extremely nimble: Spelbush and Brelca lowering Fistram down on to the stair below and then using his shoulders as a stepping-stone to join him. They reversed the process, of course, when they wanted to go up instead of down.

They soon found themselves on the first floor landing and, after tiptoeing past the open door of the dining-room where they could see Millie, hard at work as usual, they moved on into the cosy parlour.

"Up there! Look!" said Brelca, pointing up at a large bowl of fruit on a polished side-table. There were rosy-red apples, luscious mellow pears, a bunch of ripe bananas, and both black and green juicy grapes cascading over the rim of the cut-glass bowl.

Fistram's mouth began to water in anticipation of the feast to come.

The route up to the table-top was difficult but not by any means impossible. They set off, Spelbush leading the way, Brelca next, and Fistram bringing up the rear. On to an embroidered foot-stool first; next up on a rosewood sofa via its carved leg; from thence on to the sofa's padded arm from which it was a simple task to haul themselves up on to the table-top. They crossed the highly polished surface carefully, for fear that they might slip and slide over the edge. But as they drew closer to the centre of the table they relaxed.

Their spirits rose.

The high-piled fruit in the cut-glass bowl loomed above them.

Fistram reached up and tugged down a big fat juicy grape for himself. He held it for a moment in both hands, savouring the joys to come, then raised it to his mouth and sank his teeth into the fruit—only to spit it out immediately.

"It's wax!" he spluttered, pulling a face.

"What a horrible trick to play!" said Brelca, who had never come across ornamental fruit before.

Before Spelbush could add his opinion, the front doorbell rang, insistently. The little people exchanged glances of concern as they heard Millie leave the dining-room and scurry down the stairs towards the hall.

The front doorbell rang again.

IO

Harwell Mincing, clutching his Gladstone bag and standing on the doorstep of the Garstanton home, reached up with his free hand and felt at his disguise for reassurance. He settled the steel-rimmed spectacles firmly on his nose and patted his bushy false moustache and beard.

The door opened and Millie, failing to recognize the caller, bobbed a curtsy. "Good afternoon, sir?" she said.

"Be so good, young woman, as to inform your master that Mr Algernon Spindrift has had the courtesy to call."

"The master ain't in, sir."

"Not in!" thundered Harwell. "Did I understand you to say 'not in'?"

"Yes, sir, beggin' y'r pardin, sir, but, no, sir, 'e ain't in, neither."

"Am I to assume then that, to all intents and purposes, your master's out?"

"That's right, sir," said Millie, cheerfully, "'e is indeed, sir. That's where 'e is, sir—out. There ain't nobody at 'ome, sir, neither—'cept for me."

"Well then!" snorted Harwell, disagreeably. "Here's a confounded business and no mistake! Deuced inconvenient too!" He took out his pocket-watch, flicked it open, studied the face, flicked it shut again, returned it to his pocket and added: "Considering I've come all this way as well!"

"Was the master expecting you then, sir?"

"Expecting me? I'd hardly be here, young woman, would I, if I wasn't ex—" Harwell broke off, suddenly, then slapped his forehead with the palm of one hand as if remembering something that had slipped his mind. "Bless me, if I aren't a perfect fool!" he announced. "Aren't I just the perfect fool, eh?"

"Dunno, I'm sure, sir," mumbled Millie, not wanting to contradict the visitor but neither wishing to call him a fool by agreeing with him.

"But *I* know, young woman—and I insist that I am!" said Harwell who, by this time, had managed to squeeze his way through the door and was now standing in the hall. "Tell me—what day is this?"

"Well, sir, I knows that yesterday was Tuesday, on account of 'ow the butcher's boy was supposed to call but didn't—an' tomorrer's Thursday, definite, 'cos it's the coalman's turn to show 'is face—so I reckons this 'ere must be Wednesday, sir, an' you may stake your life on it."

"Exactly!" snapped Harwell. "The very day your master takes his weekly constitutional in the park. I'll wait."

"Beggin' y'r pardin, sir," began Millie, doubtfully, "but I ain't allowed to let nobody in if I'm 'ere on my own."

"And quite right too—a policy with which I heartily concur," said Harwell, crossing the hall towards the stairs. "But I think, in my case, you'd be expected to make an exception, wouldn't you say? Now, show me to the parlour, young woman, and then you may go about your duties."

Millie led the way, reluctantly, up the stairs.

Fortunately, while this conversation had been taking place on the doorstep, the three little people had had sufficient time to retrace their climb from the polished table-top to the floor and had also scurried across to a hiding-place by the coal scuttle.

"'Ere we are, sir!" said Millie, showing Harwell into the parlour.

"Excellent!" announced Harwell, glancing approvingly around the room. He walked across to the fireplace and stood with his back to the empty grate, feet apart and hands clasped behind his back, almost as if he was the owner of the house. "That will be all, young woman," he snapped, frowning at Millie.

"Very good, sir," replied the housemaid, doubtfully. Then, bobbing another of her curtsys, she left the room.

But if the visitor's true identity had gone unnoticed by Millie, the three little people were more observant. From their hiding-place behind the coal scuttle, they were staring hard at Harwell's boots which, once again, they had recognized instantly.

"It's *him*!" whispered Fistram, urgently. "Harwell Mincing!"

"He's tracked us down!" gasped Brelca.

"He wants to put us in one of his cages, I shouldn't wonder," whispered Fistram with a shudder.

"Ssshhh!" hissed Spelbush, putting a warning finger to

his lips and silencing his companions.

The three of them watched as Harwell Mincing moved quickly into action. First, he went to the door, opened it slightly to make sure that the coast was clear and then strode back quickly to the table where he had placed his Gladstone bag. Opening the bag, Harwell took out one of the tiny "man-traps" he had previously demonstrated to his sister. Then, after setting the cruel device, he attached it by its fine silver chain to the leg of a chair in a corner of the room.

The Lilliputians exchanged puzzled glances, unsure as to what the unwelcome visitor was up to—apart from no good!

Harwell had just taken another of the traps out of his bag and was about to set that too, when he heard the front doorbell ring. He frowned, angered at this interruption to his plans, and again crossed to the door which he had left slightly ajar. Tiptoeing out on to the landing, he peered down over the banister-rail into the hall below where Millie had just opened the door to admit her employer, Mr Garstanton.

"Back already, sir?" said the housemaid in some surprise.

"I sometimes think, Millie," said Mr Garstanton, not unkindly, "that you'd lose your head if it wasn't held on safely beneath your cap!"

"Beg pardin, sir?" said Millie, more puzzled than before, one hand fluttering up, instinctively, to make sure that her head was in its customary position.

"You let me set off for the park without my bread!" said Mr Garstanton.

"Bread, sir?"

144

"For the ducks on the lake! I *always* take the ducks some bread when I visit the park."

"But, sir—"

"It's all right, Millie. I'll get it myself," said Mr Garstanton, moving down the hall towards the door to the kitchen.

"But, sir, there's a gentleman called to see you, sir."

"Gentleman? I wasn't expecting any callers."

"Mr Garstanton, is it?" Harwell Mincing had hurried back into the parlour, retrieved his Gladstone bag and was now coming down the stairs, his hand outstretched. "Mr *Ralph* Garstanton?" he said, approaching the photographer and passing, on his way, the housemaid who was already scurrying towards the kitchen.

"Do I know you, sir?" said the photographer.

"Algernon Spindrift, sir," replied Harwell, quickly making up his story as he went along. "Didn't Mr Heppenstall mention my name to you?"

"Heppenstall?" replied the bewildered Mr Garstanton, having never heard of the name in all his life.

"Hepplewhite Heppenstall, from Heptonstall. He speaks most highly of yourself. Indeed, I am here on Mr Heppenstall's highest recommendation. Not only does he talk of you yourself in the highest terms, sir, but he has also nothing but praise and adulation for your work."

"Oh, *that* Hepplewhite Heppenstall!" replied Mr Garstanton. It was slowly dawning on the photographer that his visitor had come to have his portrait taken. Business was not too good at that moment and the children's grandfather was not going to allow a possible customer to slip through his fingers just because he didn't know who Hepplewhite Heppenstall was! "I know the gentleman very well indeed! You're here with regard to a studio portrait then? Was it a likeness of yourself alone, Mr Spinshanks, or a family group?"

"Spindrift is the name, sir, and it was only for myself," said Harwell, edging towards the front door. "But knowing what a busy fellow you must be—I'll ask no more than that my name go into your appointments book—and I'll take up no more of your valuable time."

But the photographer had no intention of letting his visitor escape so easily. "My dear sir," he said, taking a firm grip on Harwell's elbow, "if you are here on the recommendation of my old friend . . . what did you say his name was again?"

"Heppenstall," murmured Harwell, none too happily. "Hepplewhite Heppenstall."

"Of Heptonstall, of course!" beamed Mr Garstanton.

Up on the landing, Fistram had come out of the parlour and was watching through the banister-rail. As the children's grandfather led the still protesting Harwell Mincing off into his studio, Fistram ran back into the parlour to give his report to his two companions.

"He isn't out of the house yet," announced Fistram. "The grandfather's taken him into—" He broke off as he realized that Spelbush and Brelca were no longer standing where he had left them. Looking around the room, he spotted them at last underneath the chair in the corner.

They were gazing solemnly at the open jaws of the "mantrap" that Harwell had attached to the leg of the chair. At close quarters, its purpose was all too obvious.

"Look at that!" said Spelbush as Fistram joined his two friends. "That was meant for us. If he had not been interrupted, I fancy he meant to lay more of them."

"The man's a total monster," announced Brelca soberly.

"Come along, you two!" said Spelbush, turning and striding purposefully towards the door.

"Where to?" asked Fistram.

"Downstairs, of course," replied Spelbush, pausing in his stride and pulling himself up to his full fifteen centimetres. "We're going to find some means of cutting Mr Harwell Mincing down to size!"

Meanwhile, inside the studio Mr Garstanton was securing Harwell by the back of his head and body into the complicated system of clamps that would hold him still in the chair while his picture was taken.

"I still say that I could easily call back again tomorrow," murmured the unhappy Harwell.

"And I still say, sir, that I won't hear of it!" replied the photographer, giving the screw that secured the clamp on Harwell's head another tight turn. "There? Is that comfortable?"

"Not at all!" groaned the unfortunate showman, pinioned now at hand, foot and head.

"Don't worry—this won't take much more than a moment!" And, so saying, Mr Garstanton ducked underneath the black velvet cloth to peer into his camera.

It was while the photographer was under his cloth, looking into his camera-plate, that the three little people entered through the partly open door. Harwell Mincing, unable to move so much as a muscle, was also unaware that the three Lilliputians had come into the room.

Spelbush, as always, assessed the situation speedily and a plan sprang into his mind. He whispered a few brief words to Brelca, informing her of the role that she was to play in his scheme. Brelca listened carefully, nodded, and then sped from the room as Spelbush and Fistram looked for a safe place to hide.

Just in time. The two little men had barely squeezed themselves beneath a cupboard when Mr Garstanton came out from underneath the black cloth.

"An excellent pose, Mr Spinshaft!" exclaimed the photographer, clasping the rubber bulb which controlled the camera's time exposure

"Spin*drift*!" hissed Harwell through clenched teeth.

"I beg your pardon?"

"My name is Spin*drift*!"

"Isn't that what I said? No matter. I'm ready to take your portrait now—if you'll just keep perfectly still . . . "

Poor Harwell was hardly in a position to do otherwise!

But before Mr Garstanton could depress the time-exposure bulb, a bell began to jangle insistently in the kitchen. The photographer waited for several seconds in the hope that the distraction might cease, but the ringing continued loud and long.

Mr Garstanton sighed and put down the rubber bulb. "I shan't keep you a moment," he said apologetically.

As he came out of the studio, he met Millie who was

rubbing her hands on her apron as she scurried along the hall.

"Is that someone at the front door?" asked Mr Garstanton.

"I'm just on me way, sir," replied the housemaid.

But when she opened the door she found, to both her own and her employer's surprise, that there was no one outside. Millie glanced up and down the street. There was not a soul in sight.

"Funny!" she murmured, closing the door and turning back to Mr Garstanton. "I'll bet it's them street-ragamuffins up to their tricks and devilments again!" she said.

But if it *was* someone playing tricks on them, it was someone doing it *inside* the house, for now a bell with a different tone had begun to jangle ceaselessly.

"Isn't that the dining-room bell?" asked the puzzled Mr Garstanton.

"It certainly *sounds* like the dining-room bell, sir, now that you asks—but there ain't nobody in there! Leastways, not to *my* knowledge."

Millie had barely set off up the stairs to investigate the mystery when yet *another* bell began to ring out noisily.

"That there's the parlour bell, sir!" exclaimed Millie, glancing over the banisters. "And there ain't nobody in there neither!"

Mr Garstanton set off up the stairs to join Millie in her investigations.

The reason for these curious happenings, however, was not to be found up on the first floor but down in the kitchen.

It was Brelca who was causing all the commotion. Doing just as Spelbush had told her, she had made her way down to the kitchen and, once there, had clambered up on to the row of bells that were connected to the bell-pulls in all the rooms in the house. Brelca was having a rare old time of it, running along the ledge beneath the hanging bells, ringing first one, then skipping on to the next and then jangling the one that followed.

Mr Garstanton and Millie meanwhile ran from room to room, passing each other on landings and stairs as they tried to locate the cause of the bell-ringing.

"Spare bedroom!" cried Mr Garstanton, passing Millie on the first-floor landing.

"Back parlour!" cried Millie, passing her employer on the second flight of stairs.

It was, of course, all part of Spelbush's ingenious plan to get Fistram and himself alone in the studio with Harwell Mincing.

And it had proved a total success.

Secured in the chair by the photographer's clamps, the cruel showman was completely at the mercy of the two little men. While Mr Garstanton and the housemaid ran all over the house in their fruitless search for the invisible bell-ringer, Spelbush and Fistram advanced unseen on the luck-less Harwell. Spelbush had armed himself with a sharp nail he had found on the studio floor; Fistram was wielding a stout stick he had acquired from the studio's photographic scenery.

Together they began their attack on the luckless Harwell.

Fistram struck him across the shins repeatedly with the cane while Spelbush jabbed the point of the nail into his calves, time and time again.

"Stop it! No, stop it, you evil monsters!" cried the unhappy showman, for although he could not see his tormentors, he had guessed who they were. "You'll pay for this, you devilish demons . . .! No! Ow! *Ouch!* Oh! Stop it! Oh, please, *no*! Help, I say!"

But his cries went unheard, drowned by the continual ringing of all the household bells.

Then, as suddenly as it had begun, the ringing stopped. Which was probably just as well, for both Fistram and Spelbush were breathless from their exertions. Harwell too had had punishment enough and sat in his chair, still clamped and groaning miserably: "No more! No more, I beg of you!"

Outside the studio, on the first-floor landing, Mr Garstanton and Millie exchanged more puzzled glances.

"What on earth was all that about?" asked the photographer.

"If you arst me, sir," said the housemaid, darkly, "I thinks 'as 'ow it might 'ave bin ghosties!"

"Nonsense, Millie!" replied Mr Garstanton. "This house certainly isn't haunted. I'm sure there must be some quite natural reason. At any rate, and whatever it was, it seems to have ceased. We can both go about our business." With which, he set off down the stairs.

Spelbush and Fistram were out of sight again when Mr Garstanton walked back into the studio. Harwell's eyes swivelled wildly from side to side as the photographer crossed the room, quite unaware of the condition of his sitter.

"Extraordinary goings-on!" said Mr Garstanton. "As if we had experienced some sort of psychical phenomena . . ." He broke off as it occurred to him at last that all was not well with his client. "Are you all right, Mr Spinsilk?"

"Spin*drift*," moaned Harwell. "Algernon Spin*drift*."

"Wasn't that what I said?" asked the photographer.

"It makes no matter," sighed the showman. "Nothing matters any more—only let me out of here, I beg you! Unfasten me. Release me from this torture chamber!"

"I shan't detain you a moment longer than is necessary, I assure you," said the photographer. "If you are ready now to have your portrait taken, then I am ready to take it!"

"Anything! Anything you say! Only be quick about it and get me out of these shackles!"

"I'll just make sure again that the pose is right," said Mr Garstanton, ducking once more beneath his black velvet square.

Harwell Mincing closed his eyes, gulped, and hoped against hope that his agony would soon be over.

But Spelbush and Fistram had not quite done with their enemy. When Mr Garstanton had returned, they had sought refuge in Harwell's Gladstone bag. Whilst in there, they had come across his collection of tiny man-traps. Now, while the photographer fiddled about beneath his velvet cloth, the two little people came out of the bag carrying, between them, one of the traps.

As Spelbush shinned up the back of the chair, carrying with him the free end of the fine silver chain to which the trap was attached, Fistram remained on the floor where, with the aid of the nail which he had previously used to torment Harwell, he managed to force open and set the man-trap's jaws. Once the trap had been set, and Spelbush had succeeded in clambering up on to the back of Harwell's chair-seat, he hauled on the silver chain and slowly drew the trap up on to the chair beside him.

"Well now," said Mr Garstanton, appearing from underneath the velvet cloth and unaware of all this activity, "if I might trouble you for the last time, Mr Spinworthy—come now, compose your features into a smile that I may capture it for posterity!"

Harwell, truth to tell, felt not one little bit like smiling—but for the sake of getting everything over and done with quickly, he managed, weakly, to lift the corners of his mouth.

"Excellent! Excellent, Mr Spintop!" cried the photographer, holding up his exposure bulb. "Hold it just like that!"

But at the very same moment that Mr Garstanton pressed his bulb, Spelbush jammed the man-trap up against Harwell's behind.

"*SNAP*!"

"EeeoooOOOWWWAAGGHHH!"

Harwell Mincing cried out aloud as the metal teeth bit home. The pain was so intense that he leapt from his chair, dragging himself free of all the clamps and screws.

"Dear me, that won't do at all!" exclaimed the photographer. "You really must sit still!"

But the anguished Harwell was not even listening. Pausing only to snatch up his Gladstone bag, he rushed from the studio in agony, the man-trap still fastened securely to his backside.

Mr Garstanton hurried across to the door of the studio and called down the hall to the fast disappearing showman. "I don't think I captured your likeness at all that time, Mr Spindrift! I fear we may be required to do it all over again!"

But Harwell Mincing was not even aware that, for the first time, the photographer had managed to pronounce correctly his assumed name. The front door slammed shut behind the showman before Mr Garstanton had finished speaking.

Along the hall, Spelbush, Fistram and Brelca, reunited, were congratulating each other on the success of their joint operation.

Out in the street, Gerald and Philippa, returning from their piano lessons, were surprised to see a curious figure running hard along the pavement in their direction. It was a tall man dressed in black and carrying a Gladstone bag. It occurred to the children, separately but at the same time, that they had seen the man somewhere before. But neither of them could remember where. As they stood aside to let the hurtling figure past, it also seemed to them both that the man looked as if he might be in pain. But he was running far too fast for them to have time to ask him if there was anything that they could do to help.

He seemed to be running away from something.

There was only one thought on Harwell Mincing's mind: to put as much distance as possible between himself and the Garstantons' home. It would be a long time before he would go hunting Lilliputians again!

II

"I've seen it! I've seen it!" cried Philippa, bursting into the nursery one afternoon and interrupting Gerald and the Lilliputians at their game of tiddly-winks.

"Seen what?" said Fistram, poised on the nursery table with his tiddly-wink counter held in both hands.

"The ship that you're always talking about. One that's real and just your size and not a toy. I've seen one in a window!"

"Is it strong enough to sail across eight oceans?" asked Spelbush.

"Has it got lots of cabin space?" asked Brelca.

"Has it got a hold big enough to carry all the provisions we would need?" asked Fistram.

"Yes! Yes! Yes!" said Philippa, nodding her head excitedly in answer to all three questions.

"Where did you see it?" asked Gerald.

"Just now—when I was walking back from the shops with Millie. Oh, do stop asking questions! Put on your overcoat, Gerald, slip the three of them into your pockets and we'll *all* go and look at it now. Only do *hurry*!"

"Won't it wait until we've finished this game?" said Fistram, having just flipped his tiddly-wink counter into the cup and thinking he stood a good chance of winning.

"No," said Spelbush, who had not scored anything so far and knew that he had a good chance of coming last. "Do as your sister says," he went on, turning to Gerald. "Put on your coat and put us in your pockets and we'll go and inspect this vessel immediately."

Minutes later, they were on the way to look at the ship that Philippa had discovered, the Lilliputians safely hidden in the bulky pockets of Gerald's overcoat. Philippa chattered on enthusiastically about her find as they hurried through the streets.

The sailing-ship was everything and more that Philippa had said. It was balanced on a stand in the window of an office of the Blue Star Shipping Line, situated in a back street about half a mile from where the Garstantons lived.

"There!" said Philippa, holding Brelca up against the window-ledge so that she could look inside. "What did I tell you?"

The ship was complete with ropes and sails and rigging and spars and wheel and anchor. There were three planked decks, lots of fitted cabins and a hold for storing supplies. It was just the right size for a crew of Lilliputians and, most important of all, it was certainly *not* a toy.

"It's perfect!" gasped Gerald, who was holding Spelbush in one hand up against the window and Fistram in the other.

"Perfect!" echoed Spelbush.

"In every possible way!" added Fistram.

"But I shouldn't think that we could possibly afford to buy it," said Gerald, doubtfully.

The children pressed their noses against the window and gazed, long and hard, at the vessel on display. The little people did the same.

Inside the office, which was separated from the window by a red-velvet curtain, the assistant manager, Algernon Grimthorpe, was dictating a letter to his lady typist, Miss Tweedle.

". . . In conclusion, sir, it has always been this company's policy to recommend to its clients the romance of the sailing-ship in preference to the current ill-advised cult for steam-ship travel," said Mr Grimthorpe. "In short, to see a full-rigged schooner, its sails full of wind—"

Mr Grimthorpe broke off from his dictation to glance over the velvet curtain, fondly, at his pride and joy, the model clipper in the window.

Algernon Grimthorpe smiled proudly.

His smile faded as he caught sight of the two children with their faces pressed against the glass, breathing their hot breath on his window! Happily, he was too annoyed at what he saw to glance further down where three smaller faces also breathed against the glass.

"Shoo!" mouthed the assistant manager at the children, and: "Go away at once!" he added.

Algernon Grimthorpe who, it should be said, was full of his own importance, turned back into the room. "Where was I, Miss Tweedle?" he asked.

"'Full of wind', Mr Grimthorpe," replied Miss Tweedle.

The assistant manager frowned again and shot a suspicious glance at Miss Tweedle. But the lady-typist looked back at him, innocently.

"Harrumph!" went Mr Grimthorpe, clearing his throat disapprovingly, but he decided to drop the matter and continue with his dictation. ". . . a full-rigged schooner, its sails full of wind, is a far finer sight than that of a blackened steamship emitting clouds of smoke and propelled through the ocean, or so its devotees would have us believe, powered by nothing but hot air—"

Mr Grimthorpe broke off again as he glanced over the velvet curtain for a second time.

"Well I never!" he murmured to himself. Those dreadful children had not budged an inch and were still outside, breathing on his window. "Clear off!" he mouthed at them, waving his hand angrily to speed them on their way. This time, thank goodness, it did seem as if they were moving on.

"And about time too!" said Mr Grimthorpe to himself and, turning back to his typist, he said aloud: "What was I saying, Miss Tweedle?"

"'Nothing but hot air', Mr Grimthorpe," replied the lady.

This time, the assistant manager thought he *did* detect a trace of a smile on the typist's face. Before he could pursue the matter though, the bell rang above the door as it was pushed open from outside.

"My goodness gracious!" murmured Algernon Grimthorpe to himself, as Gerald and Philippa walked in. "It's those dreadful urchins who were dirtying my window with their breathing!" And he settled himself at his desk, not wishing to have anything to do with the children.

Miss Tweedle, however, was much more obliging. "Good

afternoon," she said with a bright smile as Philippa approached the counter. "And what can I do for you today?"

"We were wondering about the ship you've got in the window?" said Philippa, casting a backward glance at Gerald who had moved towards the velvet curtain.

"The *Crimea*?" said the typist. "She's an Atlantic schooner. What was it you wished to know about her?"

"We . . . we were wondering how much it would cost?" replied Philippa, hesitantly.

"Well now, that would all depend, wouldn't it," began Miss Tweedle, helpfully, "upon the time of year, for one thing—and there are different classes . . ." While she was speaking, the typist had taken out a thick timetable and was now thumbing through the many pages.

With Miss Tweedle thus engaged, and while the unfriendly assistant manager was busy at his desk, Philippa sneaked another glance at her brother. It was Gerald who had successfully smuggled all three of the little people into the shipping office in his pocket. He was now lifting up the bottom of the velvet curtain and, one by one, slipped the three Lilliputians underneath it into the window.

Once inside the window, Spelbush, Brelca and Fistram clambered up on to the deck of the *Crimea*. They wanted to make sure that the ship would fulfil their requirements: that it could be trusted to carry them across all the oceans between England and their homeland. While Spelbush tested the sails and rigging and Fistram tried the ship's wheel, Brelca went below and inspected the cabin accommodation.

Inside the office, unaware of all this activity, Miss Tweedle looked up from her timetable and smiled at Philippa. "The summer crossings are the *most* expensive," she said. "Especially if you wish to travel POSH."

"Posh?" echoed Philippa, puzzled.

"P—O—S—H. That means a cabin on the port side going *out*, and a cabin on the starboard side coming *home*," explained Miss Tweedle. "It's the way that all the grand people travel. But, of course, it is *very* expensive—"

"I'll deal with this, Miss Tweedle," said Mr Grimthorpe getting up from his desk. He stuck his thumbs into his waistcoat pocket importantly, and frowned. "You're the pair of young hooligans who were finger-marking my window pane and breathing all over it a moment ago, aren't you?"

Philippa looked at her brother for support.

"No, sir," said Gerald, shaking his head firmly. "We were only looking into it."

"And what are you doing now—standing over by that curtain?" added Mr Grimthorpe, suspiciously.

"No reason, sir!"

"Come here, boy!"

Gerald attempted to signal over the curtain at the little people but Mr Grimthorpe beckoned him with his forefinger. "At once!"

Gerald walked across, nervously, to join his sister at the counter.

Inside the window, Spelbush, Brelca and Fistram held their breaths and froze like statues as an old couple paused in

161

the street to gaze at the window. The ruse was successful. The man and woman mistook the Lilliputians for model figures that were part of the *Crimea*'s fittings. As the old couple moved on, the little people breathed again and continued their inspection of the ship.

"It's just the vessel to suit our needs!" cried Spelbush, testing the ship's wheel and discovering, to his delight, that it moved easily to his touch.

"There are *lots* of cabins!" called out Brelca from below. "There's sufficient hanging space for as big a wardrobe as we wish to take!"

"And the hold's enormous," announced a joyful Fistram as he clambered up on to the deck through a hatchway. "We could store sufficient provisions to take us twice around the world."

The three little mariners exchanged satisfied smiles at the prospect of putting out to sea again.

But inside the shipping office, things were not going so well.

"And might one enquire," began Mr Grimthorpe, looming over the children, "how you intend to finance this unlikely venture?"

"With our pocket-money," said Gerald.

"Pah!"

"And by emptying our money-boxes," said Philippa.

"Pocket-money!" sneered the assistant manager. "Money-boxes! Fiddlesticks! Is this some sort of prank? Are you deliberately attempting to waste my time?"

"No, sir." The children spoke together.

"Then have you any conception, either of you, how much it would cost—even if you travelled steerage—for two berths on the *Crimea* sailing from Liverpool to New York?"

Gerald and Philippa looked puzzled.

"*We* don't want to go anywhere," said Gerald.

"It isn't for ourselves," added Philippa.

"We wondered," continued Gerald, "how much it would cost to buy her."

"Buy her!" thundered Mr Grimthorpe. "Buy the *Crimea*!"

"Not the real one," explained Philippa. "The big toy boat in the window."

"B-b-big toy b-b-boat!" stammered Mr Grimthorpe. "That ship is not for sale, miss. Neither is it a toy. The vessel in the window is an accurate scale model—correct in every particular detail—of the proudest ship in our passenger fleet. Big toy boat indeed! Miss Tweedle."

"Yes, Mr Grimthorpe?" said the typist, nervously, getting to her feet.

"Escort these ignoramuses out of the office!" he bellowed. "What are you up to now, boy?"

While Mr Grimthorpe was speaking, Gerald had edged his way back towards the window and was standing with his hands behind him, poking them underneath the curtain. "I'm not doing anything—just standing here," he gulped.

"You are causing some sort of mischief. They only came in here to cause mischief, Miss Tweedle. Consider what Mr Mardle would say were he to come out of his inner sanctum." As he spoke, Mr Grimthorpe nodded at a door which had the

163

word *Manager* written across it in big gold lettering. "Why—how do you think he would react if he discovered that we allowed our time to be taken up by meddlesome mischief-makers? Get them off the premises instantly, Miss Tweedle—or I shall summon a constable and have them put in charge!"

But Mr Grimthorpe's angry outburst had at least given the little people sufficient time to scamper across the window, unnoticed, and into Gerald's hands. As Miss Tweedle got up from her chair behind the counter, Gerald managed to slip the Lilliputians into his pockets.

"This way, children," said the typist, not unkindly. "You'd best go quickly—or there'll be trouble, I'm afraid."

But once outside in the street, the children were in no hurry to be on their way. Instead, they stopped again outside the window of the shipping office and gazed wistfully at the sleek lines of the ocean-going clipper. Gerald fished the little people out of his pockets and held them up for a last longing look.

"It was exactly what we wanted," sighed Brelca.

"Just what we've been looking for," said Fistram.

"We'll never find another ship like it," said Spelbush, sadly. "We might just as well give up all hope of getting the feel of a deck beneath our feet ever again."

Inside the shipping office, Mr Grimthorpe and Miss Tweedle glanced up as the door marked *Manager* opened and Mr Mardle, their employer, came out.

"Mr Grimthorpe! Miss Tweedle!" cried Mr Mardle, a red-faced cheery man with side-whiskers. He was carrying a rolled-up document and he spoke in a voice that was full of excitement. "Great news! We live in times of wondrous change!"

"*Change?*" echoed Mr Grimthorpe, suspiciously, not at all liking the sound of the word.

"Change indeed!" said Mr Mardle, unrolling his document and laying it out on the counter for his staff to see. "Look at this!"

Mr Grimthorpe and Miss Tweedle gazed down over their employer's shoulder.

"Why—it's the plan of a ship, Mr Mardle," said the lady-typist.

"It is that and more, Miss Tweedle. It is, in fact, a plan of the very latest, the very finest and, what's most important, the very *newest* vessel in the Blue Star Shipping Line's fleet!"

"It's a plan of a steamship, Mr Mardle, sir," said Mr Grimthorpe, dolefully.

"It is indeed! *The Royal Princess*. And we hope she will be the first of many steam vessels that the company will be acquiring, Mr Grimthorpe. You realize what that will mean, of course?"

"Yes, Mr Mardle," replied the assistant manager, nodding his head unhappily. "It will mean noise, grime and discomfort for our passengers, sir."

"Nonsense, nonsense! Don't be such an old fuddy-duddy! It will mean *speed*, Mr Grimthorpe. *Speed!* The ability to knock *days* off the times of our Atlantic crossings!"

"Atlantic . . .?" Mr Grimthorpe looked towards the

curtained window as he spoke in horrified tones. "Do you mean, Mr Mardle, that this steamship will be replacing . . ." He left the sentence unfinished but the manager understood his meaning.

"Yes, Mr Grimthorpe," said Mr Mardle. "*The Royal Princess* will shortly be taking on all our Liverpool to New York voyages," replied Mr Mardle, nodding his head.

"But . . . but the *Crimea*, Mr Mardle . . .?"

"The *Crimea*, Mr Grimthorpe, is a vessel of the past. And, while we're on the subject, you can take that model out of the window."

"Out . . . out of the window?" stuttered Mr Grimthorpe, hardly able to believe his ears.

"Head office, in its infinite wisdom, Mr Grimthorpe, has already despatched a spanking replica of *The Royal Princess*. It will be arriving any day now and will take the place of the *Crimea* in the window."

As he spoke, Mr Mardle crossed to the window and his assistant, Mr Grimthorpe, followed him. The two men now looked over the curtain and down at the model ship. Outside, in the street, Gerald and Philippa were also gazing longingly at the *Crimea*.

"Goodness me, they're still out there," grumbled Mr Grimthorpe to himself. He tried to "shoo" the children away again without Mr Mardle seeing him. But the attention of both the children was held totally by the model schooner and they did not even notice his angry gesture.

Mr Mardle had also seen Gerald and Philippa outside the window but he was not annoyed by their presence. His mind was working in a different direction from that of Mr Grimthorpe's.

"Do you think that those children might possibly like to have it as a plaything, Mr Grimthorpe?" said Mr Mardle.

"Have what, sir?"

"Why—the model of the *Crimea*, of course!"

"Do you mean *give* it to them, Mr Mardle?" gasped Mr Grimthorpe, aghast at the idea. "Give it to those . . . those hooligans?"

"We've either got to give it away or consign it to the dustbin," said Mr Mardle. "And they don't look very much like hooligans to me. They look like nice respectable children. What do you think, Miss Tweedle?" Mr Mardle turned to the typist who had joined them at the window.

"I should think they'd be delighted to have it, Mr Mardle," said Miss Tweedle, pleased for the children's sake and pleased too at one-in-the-eye for Mr Grimthorpe. "And I agree with you, Mr Mardle, they *do* look like extremely nice children."

Mr Grimthorpe's mouth drooped open.

"Well, don't just stand there catching flies, Mr Grimthorpe," snapped Mr Mardle. "Go and ask them to step inside before they disappear."

"Very good, sir," said Mr Grimthorpe, setting off in miserable mood towards the shipping-office door.

The good ship *Crimea*, with its three-man Lilliputian crew aboard, headed out from the calm waters at the river's edge into the mainstream of the current. The schooner picked up speed as the gentle breeze filled out the sails.

On the river-bank, Gerald and Philippa were waving goodbye to their friends.

"Is it a very, *very* long way across eight oceans?" asked Philippa, who was close to tears.

Gerald nodded solemnly. "Almost all the way around the world, Phil," he said.

And now a tear *did* roll slowly down Philippa's cheek but she made no attempt to brush it away. "We'll never set eyes on them again," she said. "Never ever."

On the deck of the *Crimea*, the little people paused in their shipboard duties to wave back at the two children who grew smaller and smaller as the schooner continued on its course.

"Taking one thing with another, Fistram, I think we were extremely lucky," said Brelca. "We couldn't have wished to meet two nicer children."

"I shall treasure their friendship all my life," agreed Fistram.

"Speaking of treasure," put in Spelbush, who was standing at the wheel of the *Crimea*, "you do both realize, don't you, that we're going home without any real cargo?" He paused to steer the vessel past a broken branch that had fallen from an overhanging tree and was stuck in the river-bed. "Have you given a moment's consideration, either of you, to what we're going to tell his most imperial majesty, Emperor Golbasto Momaren Evlame Gurdilo Shefin Mully Ully Gue the Seventeenth, when he demands to know how we come to have crossed vast oceans, conquered a savage continent, and yet return empty-handed?"

"Not entirely empty-handed," said Fistram, with a sly wink at Brelca. "We are taking back with us the recipes for pink blancmange and yellow custard."

Brelca giggled aloud and Spelbush gave her a long hard look. It seemed, for several moments, as if Spelbush was about to explode with anger but he managed to keep his feelings to himself.

"Sheet home the tops'l!" he cried.

"Aye aye, captain!" Brelca called back, tugging at the rigging.

"Starboard tack!"

"Starboard tack it is, captain!" called Fistram, who had taken over the wheel.

"Seaward ho!" shouted Spelbush, striding importantly about the deck.

Far, far behind them, on the river-bank, Gerald and Philippa watched the *Crimea* disappear from sight. The children stood for a moment longer, gazing at the green weeds that waved gently to and fro beneath the clear surface of the rushing river, and then they turned and plodded off through the thick meadow-grass towards the houses and their home beyond. Gerald walked in front, head bowed, while Philippa followed several paces behind, one crystal tear still poised on her cheek. Both lost in their own thoughts, they said nothing to each other.

But if the children were still thinking about their little friends, the Lilliputians themselves had no time at that moment for thoughts of Gerald and Philippa.

"Spelbush! Fistram!" cried Brelca, who had climbed up

into the *Crimea*'s rigging. "Look ahead!"

The two little men shaded their eyes with their hands against the sun and stared hard along the river where Brelca was pointing.

Ahead of them, directly in their path, lay a danger which the children had forgotten—a tumbling weir which, to the Lilliputians, held all the menace of a raging waterfall.

"Hard to port!" cried Spelbush.

Fistram tugged desperately at the wheel, to no avail, while Brelca strove hard to keep her balance on the deck that was already pitching and swaying beneath their feet. The schooner was trapped in the fast-running under-current that was drawing it closer and closer to the turbulent waters.

"Port your helm!" yelled Spelbush again.

"It's no good, Spelbush—I can't control her!" cried Fistram.

Then, all at once it seemed, the weir surrounded them—stretching away on either side as far as the eye could see and thundering in their ears.

The *Crimea*'s prow struck the rim of the weir with a heavy blow that shook the vessel from stem to stern, staving in the hull's fragile planking and sending the rushing water into the hold. At the same time, the damaged schooner was swung round against the weir's wall where its flooding bows took the full force of the oncoming river. The ship's timbers creaked and groaned and, already, splinters of wood were breaking off and hurtling over the frothing waters of the weir.

"Abandon ship!" yelled Spelbush.

The three little mariners, shipwrecked for a second time in British waters, dived over the *Crimea*'s side into the white foam-capped waters that swirled and eddied all around them, and swam for their lives . . .

That same night, in the Garstanton nursery, an oil-lamp flickered feebly on the bamboo table between the children's beds.

Gerald was already fast asleep but Philippa lay wide-awake, staring out through the window at the moonlit sky and wondering about her friends.

Suddenly, she thought she heard a creaking sound. She looked across at the door which had not been firmly shut and she was sure she saw it move slightly.

"Gerald! Wake up!" hissed Philippa, sitting up in bed and turning up the oil-lamp.

Gerald, instantly awake, also sat up in bed and his eyes followed his sister's pointing finger.

There could be no doubt now that the door *was* moving— ever so slowly—but moving just the same.

The children looked down at the foot of the door as three little figures staggered in through the narrow opening. The Lilliputians were wet, dirty, dishevelled and exhausted. They trudged across the nursery floor and then stood, hands on hips, gazing up at the children accusingly.

"We blame the two of you entirely, you know!" said Spelbush, crossly. "You might have had the good sense to have left an outside door or window open—just in case."

"We almost drowned," said Fistram.

"We've had to walk miles," said Brelca. "Miles and miles."

"The ship's completely wrecked," said Spelbush.

"We haven't had a bite to eat all day," said Fistram.

"I've lost every stitch of clothing I possess, apart from what I'm standing up in," said Brelca. "I am going to need an entire new wardrobe."

"You should have thought to have left a window open," Spelbush repeated. "I am Spelbush Frelock, ambassador and emperor's emissary—it is not my role in life, you know, to enter houses via the coal-shute!"

After which, the three little people turned their backs on the children and set off, bad-temperedly, across the nursery rug towards the shelter of the dolls' house.

Gerald and Philippa exchanged a smile. Whatever misadventures had befallen them, the little people didn't seem to have come to any real harm. The children snuggled down contentedly beneath their bedclothes and very soon were fast asleep.

The next morning, while Gerald and Philippa were sitting side by side at the nursery piano practising the duet which their music teacher had set them, the three little people were out in the window-box, lying on the grass and gazing up at the clear blue sky.

Brelca and Fistram were separately lost in their own thoughts, solemnly considering the previous day's happenings and contemplating how their attempt at a sea voyage home had ended in failure. Only Spelbush seemed in good heart as he sang along with the piano music that was drifting out through the open window.

"Dee-dee-dee-dee-di-di-dee-dee-dah!" trilled Spelbush for the umpteenth time.

"Oh, do give over," growled Fistram, unable to put up with his companion's cheerfulness any longer.

"I can't imagine what he's got to be happy about?" sighed Brelca.

"Simply, because it is not in my nature to be defeatist," replied Spelbush, loftily. "I am what I am. What am I? I am Spelbush Frelock—adventurer—explorer—ambassador —optimist extraordinary—"

"Shut up, Spelbush," snapped Brelca and Fistram together.

"You two should learn to make the best of things," said Spelbush, undeterred. "We survived, didn't we? We're still here, aren't we?"

"Precisely," said Fistram. "Still *here*—on foreign soil. Here we are and here we'll stay."

"For ever," said Brelca, sadly. "We'll never get home again now. We're here for ever and a day."

"I keep telling you, Brelca, don't be so pessimistic," said Spelbush. "We'll get back. One day. Somehow. We'll find a way. There's got to be a way . . ." As he spoke, Spelbush put his hands behind his head, leaned back comfortably, and gazed across the roof-tops of the giants' world.

Just then, from behind a distant chimney-pot, a large and gaily coloured gas-filled balloon drifted into view. A large wickerwork basket hung below the balloon. It contained a two-man crew. The Lilliputians had heard about such things from the children. But this was the very first they had ever seen.

Mankind was beginning to conquer the skies.

"You see!" said Spelbush. "There's always something new on the horizon."

And, all at once, the spirits of both his companions rose.

"Who knows?" murmured Brelca to herself. "Perhaps one day, *we*'ll build a balloon that's all our own . . ."

"Who can tell?" murmured Fistram, softly. "Some day we may fly all around the world in one of those . . ."

But there was no immediate hurry, they decided. Any homesickness had been spirited away. After all, life in the Garstanton home was not *too* bad. There were worse things than being fed and clothed by two enormous children.

The gas-filled two-man balloon drifted on out of sight. The sky was empty now except for the golden sun which had risen from behind the roof-tops and was climbing higher and higher with every passing minute. From the street below, the sounds of a hurdy-gurdy drifted up and mingled with the piano music.

It was going to be a beautiful day.

Fistram remembered that he had heard Millie tell the children there was to be pink blancmange that afternoon for tea . . .

Brelca felt sure that she had seen Philippa sorting out scraps of cloth and coloured cottons from the sewing-basket earlier that morning . . .

Spelbush had a feeling, in his bones, that their adventures had not ended with the wrecking of the *Crimea* the day before—the adventuring had only just begun!

The King of the
Copper Mountains

PAUL BIEGEL

For more than a thousand years King Mansolain has
reigned over the Copper Mountains, but now he is old
and tired. To keep his heart beating, he must hear
exciting stories.

So one by one the animals of his Kingdom come to
tell their tales – the fierce wolf, the chattering squirrel,
and the three-headed dragon, breathing fire. The beetle
sits close to the King's ear to tell his story while the
other animals lie on his beard. Next comes the mighty
lion and last of all, the dwarf. He prophesies that the old
King *could* live a thousand more years, but only if the
Wonder Doctor arrives in time . . .

For eight-year-olds and upwards.